Sticks and Stones

Book Four of the *Coming Back to Cornwall* series

Katharine E. Smith

HEDDON PUBLISHING

www.heddonpublishing.com
www.facebook.com/heddonpublishing
@PublishHeddon

Katharine E. Smith is a writer, editor and publisher.

An avid reader of contemporary writers such as Kate Atkinson, David Nicholls and Anne Tyler, Katharine's aim is to write books she would enjoy reading – whether literary fiction or more light-hearted contemporary fiction. *Sticks and Stones* is her seventh novel and the penultimate book in the Coming Back to Cornwall series.

Katharine runs Heddon Publishing from her home in Shropshire, which she shares with her husband and their two children.

for Laura and Edward -
you make me happy every day

Sticks and Stones

COMING BACK

Even with the window open, the room is almost unbearably hot. I rub my forehead, circle my shoulder blades. Lean my head back and sigh.

Julie chuckles. "Look, there is no way you're going to be able to do anything useful today, Alice. Why don't you just take the afternoon off? Head into town, to the beach. Have a swim. It will help the time pass more quickly, and I'll actually be able to get some work done if I don't have you sitting there, fidgeting and sighing every two minutes."

I smile sheepishly. It's true. I can't concentrate today and it's not just because of the heat. Today is the day that Sam comes back to Cornwall, for good.

"Maybe you're right." I flex my hands on the keyboard, feeling the slightest of breezes teasing my face.

"There's no maybe about it. Now go on, get out of my hair. This menu isn't going to write itself, you know."

I won't be told twice. I shut down my computer, stand up and look at Julie, feeling slightly guilty seeing as she's hard at work and I'm bunking off. "Are you sure…?"

"Just go!"

It appears I will be told twice.

Amethi is peaceful right now. Even the birds are quieter than usual, their hearty chorus diminished in the heat; some of them, I know, will have left to find deeper, darker and cooler woodland for the rest of the summer. I miss the blackbirds, in particular. But in their wake, there is room for the buzzing of insects and the chirping of crickets. The long grass between the garden and the trees is alive with life: sunlight glints on tiny winged creatures darting this way and that; butterflies flit merrily over the fluffy seedheads; midges teem above the pond area, which is all but dried out.

The trees which guard Amethi are still, and strong. Beyond them lies a mile or two of land before we reach the sea but even from here, I am aware of its presence. Strong, steady and constant.

I cherish these days, when it is just Julie and me here. Sometimes, just me. When Julie has gone home to Luke, and Sam is not here, it is literally Amethi and me. I had worried I would feel scared or lonely at times, but I never have.

We said goodbye to our guests this morning and now have until Monday afternoon free to prepare for a writing retreat. This will be our fourth such event and will be hosted by a local writer, Vanessa, and her partner, Rosie. They are both writers, in fact, but Vanessa the more commercially successful. Julie and I were introduced to them by Paul Winters, who I dated a few times before getting back together with Sam for the second time. Paul has become a good friend and a great mentor for me and Julie.

On the forthcoming course there will be ten students, who will share the larger accommodation whilst Rosie and Vanessa will stay in the two-bed place. Although they live in Marazion, hardly a huge distance away, it makes sense for them to be on site. Everybody mucks in, with a rota for preparing breakfast and lunch, and washing up, although

Julie cooks the evening meal for everybody. Meals are eaten in the communal area, where we have set up the large dining table in one half of the room, and a load of more comfortable seats in the other half, creating a space to relax in the evenings, and for the laidback writing and discussion sessions during the day. The bi-fold doors will be open if the weather stays like this and the writers will be inspired or distracted by the outdoors.

We are well into our second year here now and as well as the writing retreats, this communal space is used for, variously, business conferences, yoga sessions, wedding receptions, and anything else we can think of. We are constantly learning and constantly exhausted but I am so happy and when I look out of my bedroom window in the morning, I still can't believe that this is really happening to me.

As I cross the crunchy, sun-dried gravel to my little two-bed house, I can't help but skip a little. It is a blue-skied, Cornish summer day. I know that just a short drive away, the sea is twinkling merrily, and I like to think it is waiting for me. To top it all, somewhere upcountry, Sam is in his car – piled high with all his worldly belongings – and is making his way back here, for good.

1

The beach is busy; even though it is a week day, and even though it is not quite school holiday time yet. Who are all these kids, who should surely be in school? I can't help but smile as I pass them, though. I remember exactly how it feels to be a kid on the beach; digging and discovering the cool dampness of the sand below the surface, watching the water seep through the deep darkness. The freedom; the space of the beach, and the feel of the sea breeze, gently adorning bare skin with a delicate saltiness. Lying on a towel, eyelids sun-red, listening to the unfamiliar sounds: other kids playing, seagulls shrieking; waves rolling and crashing.

I loved Cornwall then and I love it now. But still, I would like a little bit of space and so I move further along the beach, to what I now think of as my spot – not to the exclusivity of other beach-goers, but as a creature of habit, it's the place I always head for, hopeful that nobody else has got there first. I am in luck today. The small rocky outcrop jutting up from the sand is uninhabited. The tide is a long way out and has yet to turn. It will be just me and the barnacles.

I stop at the beach shack and greet Tom, buying an orange juice, a coffee and a KitKat. Another habit of mine. These three items form my very own holy trinity.

I walk on, swinging my bag gently in one hand; trying

not to spill my coffee in the other. I put the cup down on the rock and pull my towel from my bag, spreading it on the bumpy surface. And then – a little trick I've learned since living down here – I pull the camping pillow from my bag as well. In truth, this is little more than a deflated beanbag, but it does add a degree of comfort. I set it against the rock, sit on the towel, lean back and sigh then shiver as a little ripple of excitement crosses me.

It is hard to believe that this day is finally here. A day which I thought for some time would never come. When Julie and I came back to Cornwall, I had hoped that I would see Sam but I had no idea whether he would still be around and, after ten years apart, never really thought that we would get back together – although that didn't stop me dreaming.

It's been four years since then and we have been apart again, for the majority of that time. Sam has been studying in Bangor so we've been limited to occasional visits and breaks from study. We even split up in his first year away as it proved too much, with him also having his daughter Sophie to think about. And yet, despite all the obstacles life has thrown in our way, we know we are better off together. Today marks the start of what I hope will be a steadier time for us, and we can be like any other normal couple

But there are hours yet and I can't really sit still. Tucking my keys and phone inside my empty sunscreen bottle – carefully washed and reconstructed so that it pulls apart but to the untrained eye looks just like any other sunscreen bottle, which is great as long as nobody is out to nick sunscreen – I pull off my t-shirt and shorts so I am just in my bikini, and I stride across the sand to the sea. I don't hesitate before plunging into the water, which, despite the day's heat, is still stingingly cold. Ducking my head under,

I come up with the salt stinging my eyes and skin, gasping at the delicious feeling and ducking under again. Then I forge forward, strongly, through the waves, which are not much to speak of today. The usual congregation of surfers is a little way out, lying on boards but presumably accepting that today is not really their day. It is too still, too calm.

There is a buoy a little way out, which I have made it my aim to get to before I turn back. I am sure of the currents and I know that the lifeguards are great on this beach, should I ever need them. I remember Sam being cross with me when, aged eighteen, I had gone gung ho into the waves one night, trying to impress him and yet achieving quite the opposite effect. I knew then that I should have been more careful and as the years have passed I've learned to respect the sea even more. But I love swimming and I don't think anything can beat that feeling when you're far enough from shore that it is just you and the water, the sky above, and whatever creatures lie beneath (sometimes it's best not to think about that). I have a dream that I'll encounter dolphins sometime but I wonder what I would actually do if that happened. Would I freak out? They come through the bay more regularly than ever these days and I love to watch their sleek, dark bodies shimmering in the light as they propel themselves up and over the waves. If there is such a thing as reincarnation then I want to come back as a dolphin.

These thoughts go through my head as I plough through the water. At the buoy, I swim around it, take a few moments to tread water, then head back towards the shore. Now my coffee will be cold, I realise, but then the day is so hot, I'm not really sure it matters. Thoughts of the KitKat and orange juice drive me forward and before long I am back in the shallows, wading through the gentle waves and kicking a rainbow spray of seawater up with each step.

I towel-dry my hair then I lay the towel back across the rocks, allowing my skin to dry off in the sun; relishing the tiny goose pimples which prickle me briefly before I warm up.

The KitKat is gone within moments, followed swiftly by the juice. My coffee is still acceptably warm so I down that, too, then I check my sunscreen bottle. The keys and phone are still there. I lie back, trying to make myself as comfortable as possible, pull my sunglasses over my eyes, and listen to the sounds of the beach. Despite my excitement – bordering on nerves – at the thought of Sam's return, before long I am vaguely aware that I am drifting off. Twice, I catch myself before I fall asleep, then I give in.

2

"You're here already!" I practically dance across the gravel to my beautiful, golden Sam, who is standing with Julie, and grinning, a couple of bags by his feet.

"Ha! I told you I was going to set off later than I actually did!" He slips his arms around my waist and kisses me. "I knew you'd be over-excited."

"Were you in on this?" I look at Julie, who just shrugs and smiles enigmatically.

"Don't know what you mean," she says, "but it's Saturday night and I'm bushed. And I want to make the most of a day off. The menu's done, the food order's in, arriving Monday morning. I'll leave you two love birds to it."

She kisses me, and hugs Sam. I am holding his hand, feeling its reassuring solidity in mine. We wave at Julie as she drives away, leaving a cloud of summer dust in her wake, then we turn to each other.

I feel suddenly, inexplicably shy. I put my face into Sam's chest.

"Are you OK?" he asks, his hands on my shoulders, gently prising me away so he can see my face.

"Yes. I just can't believe it. You and me. This is it. We're together!"

"Yes," he kisses me. "We are."

"Living together!" I grin delightedly.

"Oh my god," he says. "Is this where I get cold feet and

8

turn all commitment-phobic?"

"You'd better not," I laugh and kiss him slowly, lingeringly, thinking of what Kate says in yoga classes about being 'in the moment'. I want to be right here in this moment; to imprint it on my mind and remember it forever. I can feel a very gentle stubble on Sam's chin as I kiss him, and he tastes vaguely minty. His hands are on my waist and he is kissing me back. An insect buzzes right past our ears and a tender breeze ruffles across Amethi, making the hairs on the back of my neck stand up. I shiver slightly.

"Are you OK?" Sam asks again.

"Yes, I really am," I smile at him and we kiss again then he takes my hand and, leaving his bags right where they are, on the gravel, leads me into our home.

The following day, Sunday – traditionally a day of rest, or that's my excuse – we sleep in. I wake first and I'm amazed to discover it's 10.37am. Sam is still fast asleep, and I leave him that way, gently opening the window further to try and create a bit of airflow. It is so still outside, and maybe even hotter than it was yesterday. A shame in a way that there are no holiday-makers here to make the most of this amazing weather but also a blessing because today; our first day as a fully cohabiting couple, Sam and I have Amethi to ourselves.

I tiptoe down the creaky stairs and pad into the kitchen; grateful for those dark red floor tiles, which are cool against the soles of my feet. I am not always so grateful for them in winter.

In the fridge is a bowl of fruit salad which Julie made; fresh pineapple, mango, orange slices, grapes and strawberries, marinating in a delicious cocktail of their own juices, and a huge tub of natural yoghurt courtesy of

Michael, the dairy farmer up the road from here. I leave them where they are for now but my mouth waters at the thought of them; particularly after last night's takeaway curry, which has left me feeling very thirsty and pretty unhealthy. Some virtuous fruit and yoghurt for breakfast should assuage my guilt.

I turn the kettle on, and take two glasses and mugs from the draining board. I prepare a pot of coffee, warm some milk, and slide a tray out from beside the microwave. I smile at my efforts as I lay everything out then take the whole lot very carefully up the narrow staircase. Sam is already awake when I enter the room; a mellow sunlight filtering through the curtains, dust motes twirling in the air. He smiles sleepily at me, rubbing his eyes.

"Hi," I say.

"Hi."

I place the tray on the bedside table and climb into bed beside Sam, feeling his warmth amid the soft covers. We smile at each other.

"Coffee?" I ask.

"Yes, please."

"Don't get too used to this," I say. "Tomorrow I'm going to be up and working and it feels like it's not going to stop all summer after that. Today is a reprieve."

"Then let's make the most of it," Sam says, and we do.

After coffee, we take our healthy breakfasts outside and sit at the small table in the garden. Sam drives into town and buys a newspaper, and some salads and bread from the deli for lunch. We spend the rest of the day sitting in the shade of a huge old sun umbrella, having dragged over some of the sun loungers from the holiday accommodation. Reading the paper and the weekend magazine, or just lying back, eyes closed, and letting it all soak in. The sunshine; the place; the reality of Sam being back in Cornwall.

"What are you grinning about?" Sam asks me.

I open my eyes slightly, squinting against the sunlight.

"Oh, just this," I say, gesturing around me. "And you."

"It's pretty perfect, isn't it?"

"Yes, it is."

"I don't know if I've ever felt quite as happy as I do right now."

I smile at his sincerity and can't help but agree.

Later, Sam produces a bottle of champagne, which he managed to squirrel away at the back of the salad drawer. We toast each other; our happiness, and our good fortune.

"It may not have all been plain sailing," he says, "but I feel like I always knew we were going to be together. Somehow. Some day."

"I like to think I always knew that," I reply, "but we've definitely had some dodgy moments. One of them lasting ten years."

"We were just kids then, Alice. And I reckon that this is how it was meant to play out."

"Maybe you're right. Perhaps we'd have got fed up with each other when we were younger. And there wouldn't have been a Sophie."

"Well, there would, but she wouldn't have been in my life," Sam says wistfully. He had got together with Sophie's mum (Kate, the yoga instructor – this is what you get for living in a small town) shortly after the summer we'd first met, and when they'd found out that Kate was pregnant Sam had, true to form, stuck around and become Sophie's dad.

Now, Sophie is thirteen – a real-life teenager – and I know she is as excited as I am to have her dad back in Cornwall.

"I don't know if I really believe everything happens for a reason," I say, taking a sip from my champagne flute, "but I do definitely believe that Sophie and you are meant to be."

"I think you're right. But I think you and I are also meant to be."

"Then you're a lucky man."

"I couldn't agree more."

With the last of the daylight, we tidy up our outside things; wistfully move the sun loungers back to the guest accommodation. Tomorrow, the real hard slog of the summer begins. I can't wait for the writing course to start; these courses are becoming one of my favourite things that we do at Amethi but compared to having independent guests, they require an awful lot of energy. Kate is doing early morning yoga sessions for the guests on Tuesday, Wednesday and Thursday, and I'm going to join these, each marking the start of incredibly busy days when I must be on hand and available at all times. I do get to participate in the writing sessions, too, which I love.

But I've been looking forward to this weekend for so long, and I can't believe today is already nearly over. The weather has made it even more perfect than I could have hoped but even if it had been raining all day and we'd been stuck inside, it would be no less special. An owl is hooting from the trees and I stand at the front door for a moment, breathing deeply. Trying that 'in the moment' thing again. There's definitely something in it but it can be hard to remember. I can hear Sam clattering about in the kitchen. A distant car. The hum of the fridge. I can feel the sea's presence, beyond the trees, and I know that not far away are Julie and Luke; Mum and Dad; Martin and David, a

12

little further along the estuary.

As soon as I came back to Cornwall I knew it was the right thing to do and I have loved living in this beautiful little cottage ever since I moved in. I certainly have no problem with being on my own but now, with Sam here, it really feels like home.

3

In the morning, I leave Sam sleeping and I try my best to tiptoe down the creaky stairs. He is exhausted, and I don't seem to disturb him. I go into the little kitchen, sliding my feet into my slippers as protection against the red tiles; it is too early to appreciate their cooling properties. Kettle on, I go to the door that leads out onto my (and now Sam's) little patch of garden. The vastness of sky is a pale blue soaked with swathes of pink. *Red sky in the morning, shepherd's warning.*

A flock of seagulls moves overhead, silently, heading towards the sea. I do miss that feeling of being right next to the sea, as I was when I lived at David's – now Mum and Dad's – house. But I can also achieve it very easily by staying at my parents' or at Julie's and Luke's. And on the flipside, it is so quiet here, even when all the accommodation is full. I know that the busy holiday season can drive Dad in particular to distraction. I certainly don't miss the tangle of cars slowly edging their way around the narrow streets, on an endless hunt for parking spaces. Out here, behind that screen of trees, it can be so incredibly quiet. Dad regularly comes to help with the garden but I suspect he's also looking for a bit of space.

The kettle is bubbling frantically now and at the sound of the click I head straight in, sloshing hot water carefully (if it is possible to slosh carefully) onto my tea bag. I pour in a little milk, retrieve the teabag and squeeze it over the

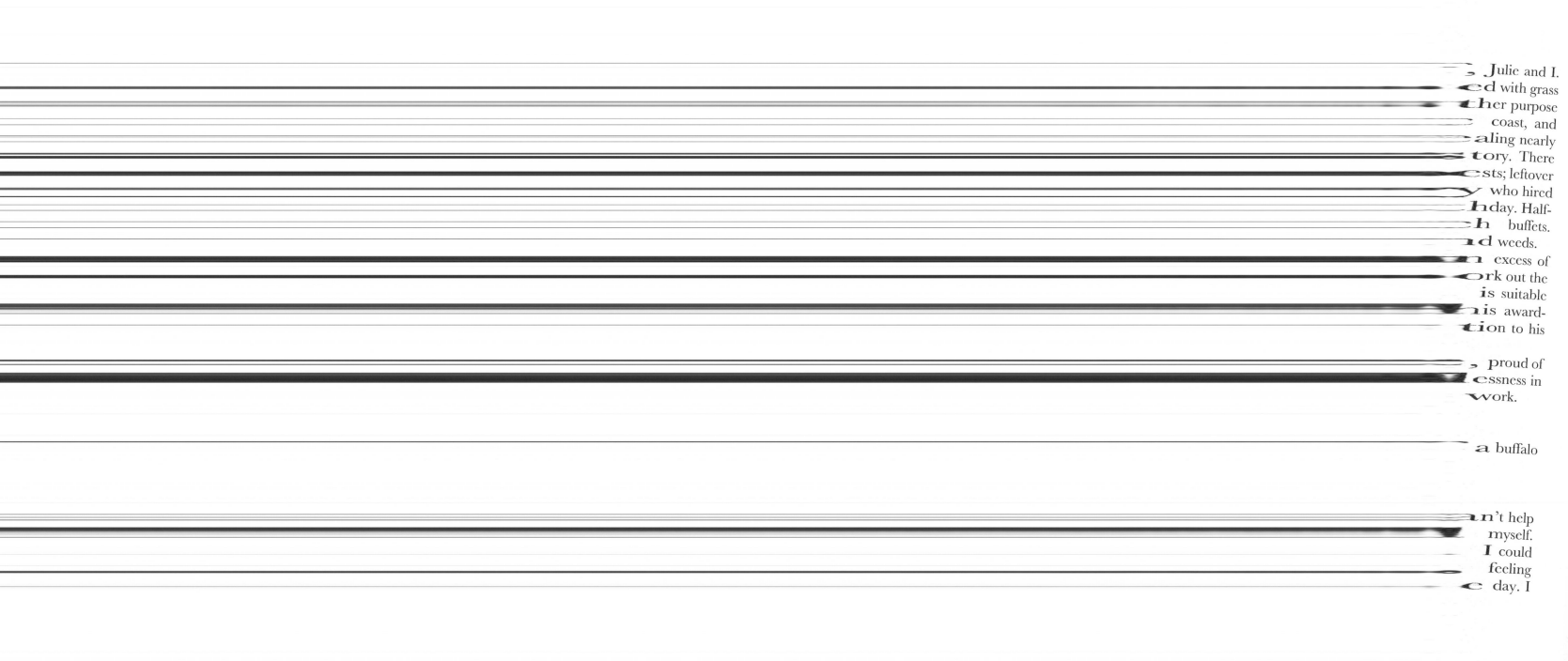

learned after the fir...

make booze free, a...

lot of writers seem t...

❖ There is no s...

close the bar at 11 ...

sometimes stay in ...

but already our m...

must do the foll...

invariably have sl...

so. Guests, mea...

communal area,

relatively tidy an...

❖ In the early

once-over, wiping...

removing all rec...

area. Then it all ...

To say that I am ...

walk from my cott...

an unpleasant exp...

of day, while it is s...

just woken up, fu...

anybody not to sn...

A sparrow flits...

another, towards

make a mental n...

The office is ab...

budget left so it is

and I to have ou...

here or a course

running of Ame...

Because of pl...

pitched roof to r...

little further along the estuary.

As soon as I came back to Cornwall I knew it was the right thing to do and I have loved living in this beautiful little cottage ever since I moved in. I certainly have no problem with being on my own but now, with Sam here, it really feels like home.

3

In the morning, I leave Sam sleeping and I try my best to tiptoe down the creaky stairs. He is exhausted, and I don't seem to disturb him. I go into the little kitchen, sliding my feet into my slippers as protection against the red tiles; it is too early to appreciate their cooling properties. Kettle on, I go to the door that leads out onto my (and now Sam's) little patch of garden. The vastness of sky is a pale blue soaked with swathes of pink. *Red sky in the morning, shepherd's warning.*

A flock of seagulls moves overhead, silently, heading towards the sea. I do miss that feeling of being right next to the sea, as I was when I lived at David's – now Mum and Dad's – house. But I can also achieve it very easily by staying at my parents' or at Julie's and Luke's. And on the flipside, it is so quiet here, even when all the accommodation is full. I know that the busy holiday season can drive Dad in particular to distraction. I certainly don't miss the tangle of cars slowly edging their way around the narrow streets, on an endless hunt for parking spaces. Out here, behind that screen of trees, it can be so incredibly quiet. Dad regularly comes to help with the garden but I suspect he's also looking for a bit of space.

The kettle is bubbling frantically now and at the sound of the click I head straight in, sloshing hot water carefully (if it is possible to slosh carefully) onto my tea bag. I pour in a little milk, retrieve the teabag and squeeze it over the sink then sling it into the little compost bin.

We are getting pretty good at all this stuff, Julie and I. We have a proper outdoor compost bin layered with grass clippings and food waste we can't find any other purpose for. I picture the compost like the Jurassic coast, and imagine a thick slice of it; a cross section revealing nearly two years' worth of food and gardening history. There might be potato peelings from our very first guests; leftover food scraps from the four generations of family who hired Amethi exclusively to celebrate a ninetieth birthday. Half-eaten wedding cake and business lunch buffets. Sandwiched between layers of grass cuttings and weeds.

After our residentials we sometimes have an excess of food, although we are learning and trying to work out the right amounts to order. But any excess which is suitable goes to farmer Michael or, more correctly, his award-winning rare breed pigs that he keeps in addition to his dairy herd.

Back up the stairs I go, one slow step at a time, proud of my ability to move so panther-like, and my selflessness in giving Sam a lie-in while I begin a tough week's work.

"Hello?"

Busted. "You're supposed to be asleep!"

"I was. I was having this really weird dream, of a buffalo coming upstairs. It was so noisy."

"Hey! I was tiptoeing, I'll have you know."

"Is that what you call it?"

I stick my head around the bedroom door. I can't help but smile. Sam, in my bed. *Our bed*, I remind myself. Beautiful Sam, from that golden summer. I wish I could go back in time and tell nineteen-year-old me, feeling forgotten and forlorn, that this would happen one day. I don't think I'd have believed it.

15

He is lying in bed, smiling at me, and it takes all my will power not to just climb back in alongside him. Just for ten minutes. No. In honesty, I am all keyed up for this writing course. I feel a sense of nervousness and excitement before these events and I need to get to the office and run through everything again, just to reassure myself. I kiss Sam and move away before his arms can pull me to him.

"You're no fun," he groans.

"No, I am a high-powered and responsible business woman."

"Damn you," he says, "you can't just keep me in your lair for whenever it's convenient, you know."

"I don't see why not." I move out of the bedroom and into the bathroom.

A quick, hot shower, and a mental run-through of events.

❖ Guests arrive throughout the afternoon, in time for a welcome talk from Julie, me, Vanessa and Rosie.

❖ Rooms are allocated and I give a short tour of Amethi while Julie cooks dinner.

❖ There is a relaxed get together after dinner, with wine and cheese and biscuits.

❖ In the morning, guests make their own breakfasts.

❖ The first workshop starts at 9.30am sharp.

❖ Lunch is at 1pm.

❖ The afternoon is free time for writing. Various locations have been designated as writing areas, including a couple of summer houses which Julie and I built, with a little help from Luke. These are the most popular spot for writers and we have learned from past experience that a rota is helpful, to ensure it is not the same person hogging them. Other spaces include the communal hall, where two or three people can easily set themselves up to work in peace. There are also benches around the grounds, and a bird hide just inside the shade of the trees, which some people like but others don't because it can be quite dark in there. I love to sit in there at times, when I need a bit of space during a busy day. Just ten minutes sitting in that little hut, keeping my eyes trained on the trees and watching a nuthatch creeping upside down, sometimes vertically; or a little gang of long-tailed tits, which remind me of children, the way they flit around together and seem to egg each other on.

❖ Evening meal is served by Julie at 6.30pm. It usually begins with olives, bread, dipping oil, etc. and is accompanied by jugs of water and plenty of wine. Main courses are always vegetarian, sometimes vegan. People don't seem to be put off by this and Julie is such a great chef, the meals are always delicious. Green Thai curry with sticky rice; lentil and spinach dahl with home-made Peshwari or garlic naan; baked aubergines with sweet potato fries; salads made with whatever fresh produce Julie can get her hands on. She makes huge vats of chutneys and pickles, which are stored in Kilner jars in the pantry. Our biggest outlay when we came here – aside from the place itself – was the kitchen, but it has proved money well-spent, and Julie had always wanted a proper country pantry. I love it, too. Walking into it, the senses are hijacked by unidentifiable, delicious smells. It always makes me hungry and despite its temperature I always feel warm in there, which I put down to the flurry of spices that I imagine dancing on the air.

❖ After dinner, the guests are free to take to their rooms or stay and socialise; more often than not, all plump for this latter option, and Julie and I open up the small bar in the communal area. Something else we learned after the first writing course; we cannot afford to make booze free, aside from the wine during dinner. A lot of writers seem to have quite a thirst on them.

❖ There is no set bedtime of course but we tend to close the bar at 11pm and then Julie will drive home or sometimes stay in my spare room. We will be exhausted but already our minds will be running through what we must do the following day. Vanessa and Rosie will invariably have sloped off at the earliest polite time to do so. Guests, meanwhile, are free to stay on in the communal area, on the understanding that it is left relatively tidy and ready for the next day.

❖ In the early morning I will come in and do a quick once-over, wiping down surfaces, mopping the floor, and removing all recycling to the bins next to the parking area. Then it all begins again.

To say that I am assaulted by bird song when I take the walk from my cottage over to the office makes it sound like an unpleasant experience. It is anything but. At this time of day, while it is still cool, the birds are active and, having just woken up, full of early morning enthusiasm. I defy anybody not to smile when greeted in this way.

A sparrow flits across my path, closely followed by another, towards the bird table outside the office door. I make a mental note to refill the feeders.

The office is above the kitchen; there was really very little budget left so it is pretty basic but it was a necessity for Julie and I to have our own space, to come to whilst guests are here or a course is running, and to focus on the day-to-day running of Amethi.

Because of planning permission, we had to have the pitched roof to match the other buildings and so the office

18

is pretty cramped on both sides. We are sitting in the caves. It gets blisteringly hot in here in the summer, and cold in the winter, and occasionally I wistfully think of the office at the Sail Loft and Bea's big desk and incredibly comfortable leather chair.

The lights flicker on in the kitchen and I get a pot of coffee on the go then head up to the office to switch on my computer. There's no point doing anything until that coffee is ready so I open up a review site, which immediately opens to the Amethi reviews; a habit I've developed, to while away the time. It feels quite vain doing this as I know how glowing the reviews are – it's almost like Googling myself – but I just can't help looking, to see if there is anything new, and to run my eye over the existing reviews for the millionth time.

We have a 4.6 'cartwheel' rating on TripRecommends.co.uk, which Paul tells us is pretty much unheard of for such a young business.

Steve from Bath says: "Like a home from home, with the addition of a personal chef. Julie and Alice are extremely welcoming and always on hand if you need anything but otherwise leave you to it. The cottage was sparkling clean, the beds were comfy, and the location is unbeatable. Two miles from the sea but far from the maddening crowds."

I like that one, although it feels like Steve might think he is quite clever.

Marilyn from Leeds says: "Spent a wonderful week at Amethi, with immediate and extended family. We booked three cottages and were able to eat together every night. Delicious food (thank you, Julie) and extremely welcoming hosts (thank you, Alice, as well). My mum loved her birthday celebration. An unforgettable week. We will be back."

I remember both Marilyn and Steve. In fact, I think I remember all of our guests so far. We've been lucky not to have had any terrible or really difficult people staying. It's got to happen sometime, I guess, but at least we've been able to build up this great reputation already. I flick over to the booking system. I know what it looks like. We are almost full until January, when we have a two-week break just after New Year, and we are already starting to fill up nicely into the following months.

I go down to the kitchen and warm some milk, retrieving one of the larger mugs from the cupboard and spooning in a little sugar. Today is going to be a long day and there is a lot to do before the guests arrive. I settle back down at my desk and soon I am lost in a world of writers and aspiring writers; running through the list of guests for this week. Checking and double-checking any medical needs or dietary requirements; making sure each has been allocated a room to suit their needs; reviewing recent emails to make sure there have been no last-minute changes. Everything looks good. Nevertheless, I am on edge, as I always am in the run-up to these events. As well as the other writing workshops we have run, we have had three yoga retreats here, which have been excellent. Kate has run these, with her partner Isaac, and the guests have by and large been lovely. Amethi seems so quiet during these weeks.

My nerves tend to die down a little on day two but until we have waved goodbye to the last guest, I cannot fully relax.

It works well with Julie and I having different roles. I am here early and she tends to come along late morning, to receive any food deliveries. When we are running a course, she will make sure everything is in order for lunch, and start reviewing the evening meal.

When we have small parties staying privately at the houses, making dinner can be a bit more complicated but we have devised a menu system. Julie prepares a menu based on what is fresh and available locally; typically having three choices for starter, main course and dessert. Guests need to submit their orders the evening before so we can make sure that we have enough of everything we need and Julie can spend the afternoon prepping. We've become quite strict about people changing their minds. It is hard work for Julie and I tend to stay out of her way wherever possible during the afternoons.

In theory, Julie arriving later than me means I get to clock off a little earlier, although, living on site, I find it hard to switch off entirely. This has not been a problem so far, though. People tend to get on with things and don't actually want me or Julie sticking our noses in. They're on holiday, after all.

After running the Sail Loft Hotel, despite the mortgage Julie and I have on this place, somehow I feel more free at Amethi. Maybe it's being my own boss. Or maybe it's the physical space which we have here. I'm not saying that it is stress-free because it's far from that but I really am happy here and I can tell Julie is, too.

Today, though, is a manic day. There is so much to do before the guests arrive. First off, I need to go through the accommodation arrangements with Cindy, who is our housekeeper and has just pulled into the car park. I go out to greet her.

"Hi, Alice. How was your weekend? Is he back?" she asks excitedly.

"If by 'he' you mean Sam, then yes. He is," I smile.

"Wow! How amazing. I bet you can't believe it."

Cindy is a little older than me; she turns forty in a couple of months' time, and she has two young children. Her husband Rod works on one of the fishing boats. He does not find fishing Rod jokes amusing. While Cindy is here in the early mornings, her mum has the kids and gets them ready for school. Cindy is then able to collect Amy and Robert and bring them home with her, knowing her work is done for the day. She is one of our best finds since starting Amethi; in honesty, Mum found her, at an Aquaerobics class.

"So what are we doing?" she asks me now, the pleasantries over – and meant, but there is work to do.

"Here." I show her the printout of the guests we are expecting, and where each will be staying, running through the details and any special requirements.

Cindy nods and hmms, her eyes running over the list, her hands taking it from mine. "Righty-o," she says, and she is off.

We have asked Cindy if she wants us to get her some help when we have busy weeks like this one. "No, I'm better working alone," she said. "But thank you."

Knowing that side of things couldn't be in better hands, I take the chance to wander over to the bird hide, to make sure that it is workable as a writing room. I'm glad I did. Somebody has left a load of leaves and grass in here. I suspect it may have been some of the children who were staying last week; it looks to me like they were trying to build a nest. I go to find a broom, and a cloth, returning to sweep the place out and wipe down the table and chairs. It is quite dark in the hide so we have rigged up some solar-powered lights. The challenge was trying to find a place with enough light for the chargers. Luke ended up climbing one of the overhanging trees, shifting precariously along one of its branches. Julie watched, an unexpectedly nervous wreck, while I directed him. On his way back, he carefully attached the wire at intervals along the branch, and to our delight it worked, although in stormy weather it's not always reliable.

I move on to the two summer houses, which also need a sweep-out and a wipe-down. I sit for a moment at one of the desks, imagining being one of the writers. Yes, I think, I'd be happy to sit here and work. I used to want to do some writing. Well, I still do, but I have to be realistic about how much time I have. I feel like I am in negative equity already, without adding something else to my 'to do' list.

Sam finds me here and smiles. "Hard at work, are we?"

"Yes," I say defensively. "Just grabbing a moment's rest."

"No need to be touchy!" he laughs. "I know how hard you work. You should grab a few moments' peace and quiet when you can. I just came to tell you I'm off to see Luke, then I'm going to head over to Penzance. I said I'd drop in today to say hello. Then I don't have to be back till next Monday." He looks suddenly, slightly, nervous.

"That's a great idea," I stand up and put my arms around his waist. Penzance is the home of the marine conservation charity that Sam is about to start work for. "They'll be glad to see you. You'll soon be a fixture and fitting of the place, you know. And you know Steven already."

"You're right," he kisses my forehead, "but I kind of wish I was starting today. I hate this feeling leading up to something new."

"But if you started today I wouldn't have you here all week."

"You're going to be busy with your writers anyway!" As he says it, I'm thinking the same thing.

"Yes, that's true, but make the most of your week off. It will fly by."

"OK. I will. I'm going to meet Soph after school and take her down to Sennen, if you don't mind."

"Of course I don't. She'll be over the moon, and it looks a lovely day for it. By then I'll be immersed in all things writing, anyway. I probably won't be home till about half ten, maybe later," I say apologetically.

"I know that. It's fine. I'll get something to eat while I'm out with Sophie. Want me to pick you up after work?"

"Well, it is a long way home…"

Sam grins. "I'll text you later. Have a great day."

He kisses me lingeringly and as he walks off he takes a route through the wildflowers, looking to me like a picture; the sun cascading down on him, amidst the myriad of colours and against the backdrop of the full, leafy trees. If I was an artist, I would paint that scene. Sadly for me, I can't paint to save my life.

The morning passes quickly once I am back in the office. Cindy calls me to go round all the accommodation and double check that everything is as it should be. I take a bottle of wine with me to leave in Vanessa and Rosie's cottage. As ever, I feel a swelling of pride in this place. The accommodation is spotless, and beautiful. When Paul had this place, he did it up to a degree; making it watertight and fixing any practical problems. Fitting carpets, and those dark red tiles which cover all the kitchen floors. He helped us source some more for the work kitchen when it came to building that. In fact, he found us the builder, too. And the supplier of materials. I don't tend to mention this to Sam too often, but I don't know where we'd be without

Paul. He has a new partner these days; Shona, a beautiful Scottish woman who lives and works in London. Nevertheless, I haven't ever quite got to the bottom of how Sam feels about Paul and I suspect it's a subject better left alone.

Julie arrives and I go through everything with her. It may sound over-the-top, running through all these lists, but it helps me to keep everything straight in my head and is also a good way to work out if we've missed anything. Today, everything seems to be in order.

"Did you have a good day yesterday?" Julie asks.

"Oh my god, yes, it was perfect. We did hardly anything," I say.

"Same here," she grins. "Remember when days like that would have seemed incredibly dull? Now they seem like heaven."

"I know. And as much as I'm looking forward to this week, I also can't wait till they all leave again! I was thinking about trying to organise a meal next week, on Sunday – once we've got all the new lot in here. With Mum, Dad, Bea, Bob, David, Martin and Tyler. And you and Luke, Sophie, Sam, Kate, Isaac… at the Cross Section, maybe?"

"Celebrating you and Sam living together properly, at last?"

"Well," I say shyly, "yes, I guess so."

"Of course you should! It's been a long time coming and god knows you've had enough obstacles thrown in your way. We'll be there, with bells on."

"OK; there's no need for bells, but if you want to ask Jim as well, please do."

"He'll be pleased," Julie says, of Luke's dad. "Did I tell you he's been seeing somebody?"

"No!" I say. "That's good … isn't it?"

"Yeah, it is. Of course it is. I think Luke's finding it a bit hard, though."

I can imagine. Luke, who is Julie's husband and also Sam's best friend, was devastated when his mum died, the summer that Julie and I came back down here. It's four years ago now but I don't suppose that makes it any easier. I am so grateful to have both my parents, and that they are still together – and happily so.

"I'll tell you about it later," Julie says, kissing my cheek. "Now, we've got writers to prepare for. And we'd better make sure they're happy – they do the best reviews!"

4

Soon after lunch, the writers begin to arrive. They are a friendly bunch, and I enjoy watching their reactions to Amethi; firstly as they arrive and get out of their cars, and secondly as they reach their allocated rooms. From my office window I can see the car park and I give each new guest a moment or two before I go to greet them.

There are four women and three men. I go through the same basic information with them, showing them to their personal accommodation, and I wait until all have arrived and had some time to settle before giving them a group tour, and introducing them to Julie, who is hard at work in the kitchen. This is a chance for the writers to meet each other, as well. Two of the women, Ann and Sheila, have met before, on another writing course. They greet each other with surprised laughter and proceed to pour criticism on their previous week together.

"Those bedspreads…" groans Sheila. "Straight out of the 1970s!"

"Oh, and wasn't the food awful?" Ann laughs.

"Remember the shepherd's pie!" Sheila exclaims, then turns to the rest of us. "I'm sorry, to sound so horrible, but the cooking there was just atrocious! This shepherd's pie… the potato was just undercooked lumps, barely mashed at all, and the layer of mince was about two millimetres thick."

"Yes!" Ann snorts. "I don't know where they got their

cook from. I'm sure your lady, Julia is it, will be much better," she quickly adds.

"Julie," I say, smiling so that I hope I don't sound too uppity, "is my business partner and one of the best chefs in the county."

There's something about the way these two are so free to criticise which has irked me – and the reference to Julie as my 'lady'. I am always over-sensitive to what people have to say about Julie and probably this assumption that she is an employee rather than co-owner of the business would have been made if she was white. Thankfully, Julie hasn't encountered too much in the way of racism in her life but there has been regular 'casual racism' throughout, which she laughs at but which drives me absolutely mad.

It is therefore very welcome when Tony – the youngest member of the group – says, "That looks like a serious kitchen she's got there. And whatever she's cooking smells awesome."

"Yeah, I can't wait for dinner," says Colin, with a twang of a Brummie accent, which reminds me of home; or, I should say, my roots. Cornwall is home now – but my attachment to the Midlands, where I was born and brought up, will never break.

"I can't believe this place," says Tony. "And you and Ju... your business partner... are so young. You've really landed on your feet."

I smile through slightly gritted teeth. People often comment on how lucky we are, without seeing all the work we had to do to get here – and continue to do in order to stay. Anyway, who is Tony to judge if we've landed on our feet? He knows nothing about us. "Well, yes, we're definitely really lucky but it does kind of mean work and life are one and the same thing."

28

"Especially for you, Alice, if you live here as well?" Colin suggests.

I smile gratefully. "Yes, I do try to make sure I get out and about on Sundays, when our guests have to fend for themselves. But even then, I'll have made sure they've got everything they need, and made any arrangements they've requested – and I have to have my mobile switched on and close by at all times, just in case."

"I see what you mean," Tony looks slightly abashed.

We continue the tour. They all love the summer houses.

"Previous groups have worked out a rota for the use of these, they've proved so popular. Julie and I would like to build a couple more at some point."

"Bagsie first go," Ann says, only half-joking.

I smile, relieved that Vanessa and Rosie manage this side of things.

Colin loves the bird hide. "I'm a bit of a birder, I must confess, and the idea of writing in here is just heaven."

"It's a bit dark for me," says Sheila.

It would be, I think – but tell myself to stop judging people so quickly.

Everybody else seems ready to be pleased, and they exclaim at all the right places, at the things I always hope they will. The communal space is looking lovely, with vases of tall, fresh crocosmia from the masses in the garden, interspersed with fronds of greenery, on the windowsills, and the seating area managing to look both cosy and spacious at the same time.

"We will have morning yoga sessions in here if the weather is bad – it's easy enough to shift things around to create some space – or, if this dry spell continues, outside. It is entirely optional but I know a lot of our previous guests have said they find it has really helped them."

29

"That's one of the reasons I chose this course," Helen says shyly. "I've been reading a lot about the effect of yoga on creativity and since I started going to regular classes, I've written so much."

"Our instructor, Kate, is lovely – and I have to say, if you get to do it outside, it's just amazing," I say. "The birdsong at that time of day is almost overpowering!"

"I can't wait!" Phoebe says and I smile at her. This is the kind of guest I like. But really, each to their own – and I am sure that Ann and Sheila won't find too much to complain about here. Certainly not the food.

I leave the group in the communal area and go through to the kitchen, where Julie has prepared some trays of fresh scones with pots of jam and thick, gloopy clotted cream. Together, we carry them through.

"A proper Cornish welcome!" Julie smiles widely and the group murmur appreciatively.

I bring through cups and saucers and jugs of milk, while Julie makes pots of tea, then I open up the bi-fold doors, and let the outside in. "Just leave your things here when you've had enough, we'll clear up as it's the first afternoon. Then we'll meet back here for pre-dinner drinks at six, with dinner served at six-thirty. Is that OK?"

"Perfect," Sarah smiles at me and the others all agree.

I head back to the cottage for a break, and a bath, before it's time to rejoin the group. These weeks are exhausting as they require me to be switched on to 'host mode' most of the time – so an hour to myself here and there is very welcome.

I smile as I walk through the door and see signs of Sam already encroaching on the place. A pair of trainers left in the hallway, and a hoodie slung on the back of one of the chairs. He is still out and I'm perfectly happy to have the place to myself for a while. I fill a pint glass from the kitchen tap and go upstairs to run the bath, lying on my – *our* – bed and listening to the rushing water.

I open the bathroom window wide, peering out carefully before stripping off and stepping into the bath. I don't want one of the writers inadvertently catching an eyeful.

I sigh as I ease myself into the water. Not too hot today, because the air is hot enough. I wish for a moment that I could go into the sea instead but that will have to wait. I promise myself to make time for an early morning swim at the weekend. Maybe on Sunday, to work up an appetite for lunch.

It's nice to have to make no effort at all. Just lie back in the bath and let my muscles relax, and my mind unwind. These short spells of time are important in this line of work because they give me a chance to refresh myself, and then I can be at my best for the guests.

I hear the click of the front door. "Hello?" called up the stairs.

"Hello," I smile. "I'm in the bath."

Footsteps on the wooden staircase, and Sam's head appears around the door. "Well, hello," he grins. "Is there room for me in there?"

"I wish," I say, "but I can't be distracted right now. I have about fifteen minutes before I need to get out and dressed. Vanessa and Rosie will be here soon."

"Disappointing," he smiles.

"I know. Very. This is what you get for attaching yourself to a very busy and important businesswoman."

"I always knew there'd be a heavy price to pay." Sam closes the toilet seat and sits down.

"How was the office?" I ask.

"All good. I saw Steven, and he asked if I could start this

31

week. I think he was joking…" he muses.

"Nice to know you're wanted!"

"Yeah, and they've got so much going on. They've just got a load of funding from the Lottery, for an education project, and Steven wants me to get involved in that. You know, for locals and tourists. It's going to be the main focus of the summer; means having to spend an awful lot of time down the beach."

"How awful."

"I know," he laughs. "Nightmare. How was your day?"

"Oh, good, thanks – all the writers arrived safely, and seem to like the place."

"Of course they do, it's bloody brilliant."

"There are two women who seem like they have quite a lot to say about everything."

"That's women for you."

"I'd suggest you leave this room for your own safety."

"I'm going, I'm going… I'll put the kettle on, shall I?"

"Sounds like a very good idea."

There is just time for a quick cup of tea with Sam, sitting out in our secluded little garden and letting my hair dry in the heat, before it's back to work for me.

"Are you seeing Sophie this evening?" I ask, kissing him and reluctantly standing up.

"Yes, I'll get going soon. I'll get a bite to eat with her, too. What time did you say your thing will finish?"

"Well, that all depends on the writers, really, but going by past weeks, it's normally a late night. I won't stay up with them till past eleven, though. I'll try to get back sooner if I can." It's strange having to think of somebody else when it comes to this; until now, I've just headed home whenever. Not having anybody waiting for me, it didn't really matter. I think I like having somebody waiting for me.

"OK, well I'll make sure I'm back before then. Soph's got school tomorrow anyway but I might pop over to see Luke again, too. The other Amethi widow."

"Good idea, you can cry into your pints together."

I kiss him again and he pulls me down so I'm sitting on his knee.

He wraps his arms around me. "We sound like an old, married couple, you know."

"We do! I kind of feel like it, too, you've been in my life so long."

"Apart from that ten-year gap…"

"You were still in my life then; and in my dreams. You know that."

"You need to tell me more about these dreams," he whispers in my ear, sending a little thrill through me.

"Not those kinds of dreams," I tease, standing up and focusing my mind. "Now, you are not allowed to be a distraction."

"How about after eleven?"

"Maybe then."

I hear a car pulling into the parking area so I walk round to see Rosie and Vanessa opening their car doors, getting out and smiling.

"Hi!" I say, giving both a hug and a kiss on the cheek.

"Alice! What a perfect week for this," says Rosie.

"I know, it feels like this weather's here to stay."

"Let's hope so," says Vanessa, always the more abrupt of the two but as kind-hearted as anyone you might hope to meet.

"Are all the guests here?"

33

"Yes, they've been settling in. I asked them to meet back at six, so we've got a bit of time to run through things before they come over."

"Oh excellent, let me just go and say hello to Julie," says Rosie, heading straight for the kitchen, while I walk with Vanessa to the communal area and she tells me about the novella she is working on.

Whenever we have one of these weeks, it reinvigorates the side of me that wants to write and I come away with a renewed vigour, determined to find even just fifteen minutes a day to get some words down but so far I have failed in this. It turns out it's very hard to find fifteen minutes a day. It will be even more so, I suspect, now that Sam is living with me.

Rosie and Julie come through to join us.

Julie has saved a cream tea for Rosie and Vanessa. "I know you live in Cornwall, and you're more Cornish than we're ever going to be, Vanessa, but I've made you a proper Cornish welcome anyway."

Vanessa smiles, rising to hug Julie warmly. "I don't know about that. Anyone who makes scones like these must have a bit of Cornwall in them."

"I have to go light on the cream," Rosie says regretfully. "High cholesterol, I'm afraid."

"Oh no," I say. "That's not good."

"It's OK. I'm walking more, and eating less, which I've always known I should. The blood tests just gave me the impetus to get on with it."

"Blood tests?" Julie asks.

"Yes, nothing serious. Just the health MOT. When you two are old enough, you'll have them, too. Still some time off for you, though!"

We sit and go through the details of the week; Vanessa

and Rosie sharing their plans, which we have already discussed, and us fitting a rough timetable for meals and non-writing activities around them. Yoga, an evening visit to the beach, and a four-mile walk which begins right here at Amethi and takes us to a beautiful viewing point on the coastal path and back. It's going to be a great week.

Dinner is fantastic: a fat baked aubergine each, shining with oil and bejewelled with cloves of garlic; great dishes of garlic and rosemary roast potatoes; succulent roasted red peppers and tomatoes. There are side salads, and bread with dipping oils. I take a sneaky look at Ann and Sheila, who have seated themselves together. They look happy enough.

Dessert is a huge fruit salad, served with or without meringues. I notice that Sheila comes back for seconds, and that Rosie doesn't touch the meringues.

Julie doesn't eat with us as she is too busy; that is one downside of our roles here, although I suspect she likes being able to go back and hide in the kitchen. I almost always end the first day of these residentials with a headache. They take a lot of energy, and I am probably more uptight about them than I realise. By day two, I generally feel more relaxed.

Tonight, the conversation flows easily. Ann and Sheila seem content to talk between themselves, which is a shame, but the others are already bonding, finding things which they have in common. I love watching how these groups of people develop. There is more often than not an extremely gregarious person – in this case, Colin – who is happy to lead the conversations, at least initially, and the others tend to develop their confidence throughout the week. Helen, who seemed shy, is actually very funny and says a lot with only a few words. I am sitting between her and Tony, who seems easy to get on with. He asks questions about Amethi and about what I did before I came here.

I tell him about the first golden summer, and returning to Cornwall ten years later; mentioning Sam but of course leaving out the details about the trials and tribulations of our relationship.

"So you're back with the first man you fell in love with?"

"Yes," I say, wanting to add 'the only man I've been in love with' but thinking it sounds cheesy.

"That's amazing. That's a proper love story."

"I suppose it is," I smile. "How about you. Do you have a… partner?" I choose the word carefully, not wanting to assume he is straight.

"No, I'm separated," he says. "I married the first person I fell in love with but I think I rushed into it. I was at a low point in my life, and I thought getting married and having children was the answer. It turns out that they weren't."

"You've got kids?" I ask, not wanting to delve into his failed relationship.

"Yes, but I don't get to see them much."

"Oh, I'm sorry. That must be hard."

"Yes," he takes a breath, "but you don't want to spend all evening talking about how my life's gone wrong! Let's eat, drink and make merry."

I must admit, I'm relieved. It's not that I'm not sympathetic; but I am here for all these guests and in honesty I don't really want to get into the realms of Tony's failed relationship, as genuine as he seems.

He raises his glass of wine and I clink mine against his. "To a great week," he smiles.

"To a great week," I agree and I turn to Helen, while

Tony begins chatting to Aadil, who is sitting opposite him.

The evening passes pleasantly but I am very grateful when eleven o'clock comes round. I say my goodnights and remind the guests to lock up after themselves. Julie has already gone home. Helen follows me out, and we go our separate ways. I can see a light on in my cottage and I smile. He's back.

"Hello," I call softly when I open the door.

"Hi," he smiles, appearing in the kitchen. "I've just put the kettle on. I thought you might like a bedtime brew."

"That sounds perfect," I smile, kissing him.

"Go and sit down. Unwind for a while before you go to bed, or you'll never sleep."

I do as I'm told and I sink down onto the settee. There is not a whole lot of room in the lounge but there is a TV and a separate chair, and a tiny fireplace. Paul had already had a new flue put in and I've been able to use this fireplace during the colder days. It is ridiculously cosy. There are fireplaces in the other accommodation but we don't let guests use them. One day we'd like to get some log-burners installed, and I think we'd feel a bit happier then. The possibility of this place going up in flames because of a careless guest is unthinkable.

Sam brings through a cup of herbal tea and a bowl of dried fruit and nuts. "Sorry, I know it's all a bit too healthy but I really want us to look after ourselves. And I know what Julie's cooking's like so I wasn't sure you'd be hungry at all."

"Don't apologise! This is lovely. And you're right, I am totally stuffed from dinner. I only had a couple of glasses of wine but it's nice to have something which feels a bit virtuous. How was Sophie?"

"Great. Of course." Sam grins, pride in his daughter

37

written all over his face. "She's counting down the weeks till the summer holidays. But she's got to do work experience and she wants to come and do it with me. What do you think? I haven't even started my job yet."

"Give Steven a ring tomorrow and just mention it to him."

"I guess. God, I'd love it if she could."

"It would be amazing," I agree. "If you're doing that education programme, she could easily come with you to the beach."

"Ha, yeah, she'd love that. I'd have to remind her we're meant to be working."

"Did you ask her about Sunday? And Kate?"

"Yep, they're all coming. And I've booked a table with Christian. I said we'd confirm numbers tomorrow."

"Brilliant! Thank you." I kiss him and settle into the crook of his arm. We drink our tea quietly and before long I feel my eyelids drooping. "I'm sorry, I'm going to have to go to bed."

"I'll come up with you. And I know, you need to sleep. I promise to kiss you chastely on the cheek and let you rest."

"Ha! Thanks," I say. "We'll be getting twin beds soon."

"I don't think we're there quite yet," says Sam. "At least I hope not. Come on." He pulls me to my feet and sends me upstairs while he takes the cups and remainder of the snacks into the kitchen.

The bathroom window is slightly open and as I brush my teeth I listen to an owl hooting, somewhere in our line of trees. *I live here*, I tell myself, as I have to tell myself often. *And now Sam lives here, too.* I spit out the toothpaste and smile at myself in the mirror. Then I walk softly through to the bedroom and fall into bed. I am asleep before Sam even gets to the room.

5

The rest of the week is so full-on, I feel like I barely have time to take a breath. I go to the yoga sessions in the mornings – after having already been up for at least an hour each day, catching up with emails, answering enquiries and so on. That is one of the most exhausting things sometimes; even while we are throwing ourselves into making sure that a residential week is a success, Julie and I still have to keep things going; planning for the future, making sure we respond promptly to emails and phone calls, marketing, paying bills, etc. I tend to do more of this as it fits with my role here, and with my experience running the Sail Loft, but Julie does her fair share. So far, I've been really amazed at how few arguments we have had. I guess we know each other so well that we can see when the other needs a break or is feeling like it's all getting a bit much. It's important then to be able to take the slack a little and let your partner have a bit of breathing space. Of course, that's not always possible, and this week is a prime example of that.

I guess I'm not really getting what I should out of the yoga because in all honesty I am finding it very hard to be in the moment. My mind is already on what comes next; breakfast for the guests, and meeting up at 9.30 in the communal area – which means this room needs to be rearranged after the yoga session (I have already had to arrange it to fit us all in – it's warm enough for an outdoor class but there is quite a strong breeze coming in from the sea at the moment, which makes it harder to relax into the class). When the writing sessions are running, I feel like I have one foot in the writing sessions and one in the running of the place. But then, I am not here to write and I have to remind myself of that. Maybe I need to book a space on a writing week somewhere else, when we have our break in January.

I notice that Ann and Sheila do not make it down for yoga this first day. They were hitting the wine fairly heavily last night so perhaps they're sleeping off their excesses. Or maybe yoga isn't their thing. It's wonderful to see everybody else gathered here, though, and Kate was here early – she always is – to give me a hand getting the space ready. She is like a different person these days and I find it hard to match her with the woman I first met on the beach, when Sophie managed to spill half a bucket of water over me while I was snoozing. Then, Kate was very much about her appearance; never leaving the house without make-up, and she confided to me that she would drink every night, after Sophie had gone to bed and sometimes before.

Now, since being with Isaac, she hasn't stopped drinking entirely but I am pretty sure it's more green smoothies for Kate most nights. And while she looked pretty bloody amazing when I first met her, she looks even better now. This morning, she is positively glowing. I pull self-consciously at my t-shirt, aware that my stomach is creating a little shelf above the waistline of my leggings.

She runs through her notes, and checks her speakers are working, while the writers gather and murmur good mornings to each other, all returned slightly to the shyness of people who have only just met, now that they don't have alcohol to boost their confidence and loosen their tongues. We give Sheila and Ann a couple more minutes but when there is no sign of them, I give Kate the nod and we begin.

Despite all the lists running through my mind like rolls of till receipts, I still enjoy the hour's workout and I try very hard during the meditation at the end to let all thoughts of work flow from my mind, for just a short time.

When the class is over, the writers head off for showers, breakfast, and to make calls home, and I walk with Kate to her car.

"Thanks for that, it was excellent. I feel great!"

"You're doing really well with it, you should try and make it to some of the classes in town."

"I know, I'd love to, but I am just ridiculously busy. Which is a good thing!"

"And now you've got Sam here, too," she grins.

"Yep," I grin back. "I can't believe how much has changed in these last few years."

Kate and Sam were once together – after the first summer I spent with him, all those years ago – and as Sophie's parents they are still close. In fact, closer than ever, and I can see the benefit this has for Sophie.

"I know. Bloody hell. I am so happy now, Alice. I didn't ever think this would happen for me."

"Well, you look very well on it," I say, putting my arm around her shoulder, briefly.

"Thank you!" she smiles self-consciously.

"And Sam said you can come on Sunday? To the Cross Section?"

"Yes, we can't wait. It feels like something we should try and do a bit more regularly. I know it sounds really cheesy but I feel like we're a great big family these days."

"Do you know what? I totally agree." There is something

41

warm and inclusive about the group of people I have found myself in down in Cornwall. And with Mum and Dad here as well, it feels complete. My parents have made themselves very much at home here, which hasn't been easy, but they've thrown themselves into various activities – Dad has even had some surfing lessons – and Mum has a job working at the local children's hospice, as their business manager.

I wave Kate off and head quickly back to the cottage before I go and do the rounds, checking on the guests to make sure they have everything they need. It's a careful balance, being attentive without being overbearing.

Tony and Aadil are sitting outside, eating granola with natural yoghurt and berries, a pot of coffee on the table between them. Each is engrossed in a book.

"Morning!" I say. "Sorry to interrupt, I just wanted to make sure you've got everything you need."

"Yes thanks, Alice," Aadil smiles at me.

Tony looks up and grins. "This is so good," he says. "And can we hear the sea from here, or am I imagining it?"

"I don't know. Sometimes I think I can hear it, but it feels like we're too far away for that to be possible."

We all stop quietly for a moment but all I can hear right now is the birdsong, and the wind rustling through the trees.

"Enjoy your breakfast," I say, and carry on to the larger house, which the women are sharing. Sheila is sitting outside with Phoebe.

"Everything OK, ladies? Sorry we didn't see you at yoga," I address this last part to Sheila.

"Oh yes, I think I should try it tomorrow morning. Phoebe says it was wonderful!"

Phoebe smiles. "I wish I could do that every morning."

"I know, it's the perfect way to start the day," I say. "Do you know what would be even more perfect? A swimming pool. If I could begin every morning with yoga and a swim, I'd be a happy woman."

"We've got a pool at home," Sheila says. "You do take these things for granted."

"I guess, people get used to anything, don't they?" I smile.

"Yes. I know I'm very lucky. But my husband's away most of the time, working, which is what pays for the house, and the pool, and weeks like this."

I feel sorry for her suddenly. It sounds like she's lonely.

"I'm sure you'll be able to get this place looking really good over time," she continues, and my sympathy quickly dries up.

"Oh. Yes, thanks. I'm pretty happy with it already," I say, trying to keep my hackles down.

"I love it," Phoebe says. "Those wildflower meadows are beautiful."

"Oh, is that what they are?" Sheila laughs. "My gardener would have those in shape in no time."

"They are in shape," I say. "We try our best to make sure Amethi is wildlife-friendly."

"It's certainly that!" Sheila says and I hear a laugh.

Ann is standing in the doorway. "I think it's charming. And I'm getting a lot of inspiration for my writing, already."

"Oh, yes," Sheila gushes, not wishing to be outdone. "Me too. I mean, it's good to visit different places, and see how other people live. It would be very boring if we were all the same."

"Exactly." I smile. "Now, if you'll excuse me, I need to

get a couple of things done before the workshop."

I call briefly in at home, where Sam is taking a shower. I sneak through the bathroom door. He is singing to himself. I snake my arm into the shower cubicle and run my hand up his spine. He jumps.

"You can cut that out," he laughs, "Unless you can join me in here?"

"I wish," I say, "but I've got to crack on. First workshop starts in less than an hour. I need to get all the refreshments ready."

"OK, I'll let you off. Have a good day. I'm going to go to Land's End, catch up with some of the gang down there, I'll be back late but I guess that works for you anyway."

"Yep, it's another late one," I say, exhausted at the thought of it. "But I'll see you tonight."

I experience a slight pang that we can't make the most of our first week of living together but we have lived together before, I suppose – when Sam was down here for his third year of uni, doing practical work with the charity he's now got a job with. It's just we knew it wasn't permanent then. Now, I hope, it's for keeps.

***

Although I've been saying what hard work weeks like this are, I can't help but feel I am cheating a little, as I get to participate in the writing workshops. It is not entirely necessary for me to be there, of course, but Julie and I agreed with Vanessa and Rosie that it might be helpful, if the crowd's tough. I can't pretend it is too much of a hardship for me and as this week is about short-story-writing, I am hopeful I may be able to produce something by the end of it. It won't be polished, of course, and I won't

44

have the time in the afternoons which the other attendees have, to focus entirely on my work, but I reckon I can squeeze in a few minutes here and there.

"Our aim," Rosie tells the assembled group – who actually are easily engaged and most of whom seem to feel able to offer their input (only Helen seems reticent), "is to have something we can share with the group on Friday morning – a celebration of our work, and our week together, before we all go our separate ways."

There are murmurings of general approval at this idea. I glance at Helen, who is smiling but looking a little nervous. I know how she feels. I am not the world's most confident public speaker and I used to be incredibly nervous about speaking in public. I can't say I love it now but I have come to realise that I am more confident than I'd previously thought. Or, probably more correctly, my confidence has grown over recent years. At the networking groups that Paul introduced Julie and me to, you have to be able to at least stand up and introduce yourself, and with each time I've done this I've realised that there is nothing to be scared of. I catch Helen's eye and give her a little smile, which she returns.

The morning passes quickly, with Vanessa and Rosie each reading short stories they have written. They are both excellent orators: clear, calm and expressive. Vanessa's story is about a child growing up the youngest in a family of ten. It is sweet and funny and touching. Rosie's is about an elephant in Thailand, captured for the tourist trade. I find it brings tears to my eyes and a quick glance around the room shows me I'm not the only one. Tony is wiping his eyes, and Helen looking down at her hands. Sheila looks chastened, and I unkindly suspect she's the type of person who supports these practices; I have no doubt she is the type of person who 'does' destinations ("Oh yes, I've done Thailand now. I'm planning to do Vietnam next year.")

But Sheila is a guest here and I need to stop thinking like this.

Tony and Helen are rostered on to make lunch this first day so while the others retire for a leisurely hour, we go into the kitchen to find Julie.

"Is it that time already?" she smiles, looking up from a pile of sliced peppers.

"I'm afraid so," I say. "As you can see, Tony and Helen are on lunch duty today."

"At least you get it out of the way now," Julie grins. "Here, let me show you what there is. If you guys use this space over here, I can keep the rest of it for dinner prep. What are we thinking? Bread? Salads? Cheeses? We've just got some seriously smelly goats cheese from Michael up the road and I'd actually be really grateful if you have it today because I don't think there's space in this kitchen for the both of us."

"Sounds perfect," Helen says shyly. "Do you have some blue cheese as well? And pears, and walnuts? If that's not too demanding!"

"We have all of those things," Julie smiles at her, "and I happen to know that's one of Alice's favourites so she'll be happy. Now, did you want to poach those pears? If so, we'd better get going. I'll show you where everything is."

"Looks like it's you and me on the chopping boards then, Tony."

"Fine by me," he says. "Shall I take the cucumber, and you take the tomatoes?"

"We've got a plan."

Tony and I stand side-by-side at the spotless stainless

46

steel work surface; at least, it was spotless. The freshly washed cherry tomatoes are slippery and I manage to spray a load of seeds over Tony's arm. "I'm so sorry!"

"That's fine," he grins. "I'll just mention it in my review at the end of the week. 'The host attacked me with a tomato.'"

"What are you up to, Alice?" Julie calls from the stove, where she is heating the water for the pears. "Don't mind her, Tony. I should have told you you're taking your life into your hands if you're in the kitchen with her."

"Hey! I'm not that bad."

"Oh no? Remember your surprise dinner for Sam? The bread rolls?"

"I can't believe you've brought that up. Anyway, you weren't there."

"No, but I saw the aftermath. Bloody hell," she turns to Helen, "they were like cannonballs. We could have sunk the fishing fleet with them."

"Yes, well, I forgot to take them out of the oven."

"You don't say."

"I'm sure if you'd remembered, they'd have been delicious," Tony smiles.

"Don't you start."

I return to my slicing – more carefully this time. Once the tomatoes are chopped, I push them into two huge bowls and scatter them with salt. I tear a large ball of mozzarella into pieces and divide it between the bowls. Finally, I go out to the cottage garden, which Julie keeps beautifully, and tear off a handful of basil leaves, their scent staining my hands. I go back to the bowls and tear the leaves into small pieces, scattering them liberally over the tomatoes and cheese. I drizzle olive oil over the top of each bowl.

"Ha. Who says I can't cook?"

"I'm not sure that's cooking, exactly," Tony smiles. "But it does look delicious."

"Don't listen to Julie," I say. "I am actually an excellent cook. She's just jealous of my skills."

"I can hear you, Griffiths."

"You shouldn't be listening. Keep your mind on the job! As I was saying," I turn back to Tony, "If I had enough time, I could do all the cooking, too."

"Of course," he says. "I never doubted it."

It's a pleasant feeling, standing side-by-side with somebody, preparing huge piles of food. While Tony concocts a delicious cucumber salad, I get out the bread knife and start to slice up the loaves, which have been delivered fresh from the town bakery this morning.

"Careful with that," says Tony.

"Hasn't anyone ever told you not to anger a woman with a knife?"

I happen to look at Tony as I say this and I am sure I catch a glimpse of a fleeting expression crossing his face but I can't quite work out what it is. Fear? Anger? It smooths out quickly and I may have been mistaken. I remind myself that I don't know the people who come to stay here, and that I should be more careful. How do I know what Tony has been through in his life?

"Shall I make a start on the lettuce?" he asks brightly.

"Yes please, that would be great."

Lunch is a success and Helen is complimented on her pear and walnut salad. Her face goes red at the kind remarks.

"You could cover that up, dear," says Ann. "there are some lovely products you can get to hide your blushes."

Of course, this only serves to make Helen's face go even redder. I quickly move to take the attention away from her.

"I can't believe nobody's complimented me on how well the bread is sliced."

"Sorry, Alice!" Colin leaps in; also, I think, to spare Helen any further pain. "This is the best thing since... sliced bread."

His Brummie accent comes on strongly with this sentence and everybody laughs. I glance at Helen, who looks relieved that the heat is off her. I'm going to have to keep an eye on Ann, and Sheila. But the rest of lunchtime passes happily.

6

By the end of the week, most of the group have bonded, as those in this kind of intense situation often do. Phoebe and Helen in particular have really hit it off and have both promised to come back and meet up for another writing week, here at Amethi.

"This place is so beautiful, Alice," Helen said last night at dinner.

"And you and Julie are so young to be doing all this! You should be really proud of yourselves," Phoebe smiled. She is probably the same age as my mum, and I took her words as a huge compliment. I've loved hearing the little snippets of writing she has produced this week and I'm looking forward to hearing everybody's stories this morning. It can be quite emotional, this last day – the culmination of so many days' efforts, and the ups and downs of people doubting themselves and their abilities; taking feedback from Vanessa and Rosie, which can sometimes be hard; baring their souls a little, as they are encouraged to do in some of the exercises they have been set.

As I should have predicted, I have got nowhere near finishing a short story this week. I just have not had the time. "You need to make the time – or, more accurately, find it," said Vanessa. "Five hundred words a day. It sounds a lot but I think if you like writing you'll get into the habit. Take yourself off to one of those summer houses, for half an hour if that's all you have, every day. You'll find

50

it happening for you."

"I'll give it a go," I say.

"Make sure you do," she smiles, her eyes twinkling. "Next time we're here, I want to see what you've been working on."

There is something of the school teacher in her attitude but I like it and I probably need it. I am determined to follow her advice. In fact, I will find half an hour later today, after everybody has gone.

For Helen, I can see that the act of reading aloud is going to be her biggest challenge. I am pleased when Rosie tells me they are going to ask her to go first. "It's hard to be the first but I think even harder to sit there, knowing your turn is coming. And I want her to be able to sit back and listen to everyone's words. She'll be able to relax when it's over."

And so it goes. Helen reads quickly, her words stumbling into each other, and her face down towards her work, but her pace does start to slow naturally and we listen, rapt, to her story of a young farm boy in Wales, in the 1940s, desperate to see the world; to see the War. His family won't have it, and he won't listen to them. He sneaks onto a train, and ends up in bombed-out London. Helen's descriptions, of the journey, and the bombed streets, would have you believe she was actually there, but her age tells you that could not have been the case. The boy meets another boy, the same age as him, and they swap stories. The other boy has lost his parents, and his siblings, and is living unhappily with his aunt and uncle. He takes the young Welsh lad into an Underground station to shelter when the sirens go off. The Welsh boy returns home, seeing the hills, and valleys, space, and peace with fresh, appreciative eyes. The story ends with the other boy sneaking onto a train, bound for Wales.

Helen doesn't look up when she has finished reading; until, that is, the clapping begins. Colin even whoops. "That was excellent, Helen. You've got to get that in some competitions."

Red-faced but evidently pleased, Helen walks back to her seat. I grin at her and she smiles back. I can see that she is shaking.

I sit back and enjoy listening to all of the stories. Because Sheila and Ann have both been a bit of a pain this week – I have heard them both tutting to each other over a few aspects of Amethi, which, as you can imagine, is not going to win them any favours with me – I would love to say that their writing is awful but in honesty, it's very good. Sheila, in particular, writes very strongly and her story is about a fox; it is written from the animal's perspective, and this surprises me for some reason. I hadn't seen her as a very empathic person but her writing suggests otherwise.

Second-to-last to read is Tony, who looks very serious as he gets up. The order has been set by Vanessa and Rosie, who both know what each person has been writing about. Tony begins to read and I can tell that he is finding it as much of a struggle as Helen, although for different reasons. "I've written this in memory of somebody I used to know," he says by way of introduction and the 'used to' indicates this is not going to be a happy story. The language he uses is heavy, and passionate, as he takes the voice of the father of a man who kills himself. My thoughts flick to Geoff; the boyfriend I had after I had left Cornwall that first time. Geoff was controlling and manipulative and eventually I ended it. Some months later, he took his own life. I know that it was not my fault. I know that he had a lot of problems. But it was, and still is, hard not to feel responsible. It also took me a long time to grieve him; I didn't feel like I deserved to, having ended our relationship, but a long run of counselling sessions taught me how I could feel. I didn't go to Geoff's funeral; I didn't think it was appropriate, or that I would be welcome. I will never forget the day that it happened, though. I stayed in bed, not eating, barely drinking; Mum and Dad worrying about me while I hated myself for making the situation about me. Mum, meanwhile – I discovered quite some time later – felt guilty as she had seen how he was with me, but had not intervened. She thought that if she had said something earlier; maybe even said something to Geoff, she could have somehow stopped it from ending the way it did. Dad was angry for a long time; mostly with himself, for he had never liked Geoff, but he felt so strongly that it should not have come to a young man in his twenties deciding to end it all. People who kill themselves I think have no idea of the ripples which will spread out from their final act; I don't suppose they are in a state of mind to think like that, but Geoff's death must have affected so many people in addition to his family. It is unimaginably sad.

I think of all of the people whose lives would be affected – if even for the briefest time – if it were me, and I am happy and grateful that I have never felt the way Geoff must have felt, or the young man who Tony's story centres around.

I listen closely to his words; see him swallow hard at a couple of points. The father's language is carefully selected and structured: down-to-earth and straightforward; a man who was not able to communicate with his son as he grew up; a man whose own father had beaten him, and who took his anger out on his children; a man who bitterly regretted not being a better father and is now condemned to wishing he could follow the same route as his son but believing he should take his punishment and live the rest of his life knowing that he was to blame.

There is quiet for a moment after Tony finishes. I think we are all taking it in. He sits back down quietly, not looking up, then I catch Colin's eye and he looks at me, then starts to clap. It's like none of us are sure if clapping is the right thing after such a terribly sad story. It's clear to me that there is more than a kernel of real life in Tony's words, and I guess everybody feels the same. He's not old enough, of course, to be the father of a grown man, but somebody, somewhere in his life, has obviously been through this. I want to tell him I know how it feels. I know it would not be appropriate. And I also know that I still feel that guilt about Geoff and that if Tony knew, he might also think that I was responsible.

Luckily, Vanessa and Rosie have been very wise in their structuring of the morning's readings and we end on a high, with Colin's story. Based, he says, on his own childhood, when he would go to watch 'the Villa' with his dad and his grandad. It is a colourful, vivid recounting of life at a football stadium – giving voices to all those who work there; setting up before the game; working on the turnstiles; serving drinks and pies at half-time; and finally to a young boy sitting on his father's shoulders as they leave the ground euphoric after a Villa win. It is beautifully written; descriptive and funny, too. All of us – even Tony – are smiling as we listen to Colin and I think it is so important that we have ended on a high note.

It's been a long week, or so it seems. Our farewell lunch is a happy affair but I am looking forward to everybody clearing out now and Sam and I having this place to ourselves for the night, before it all begins again tomorrow, with the next lot of holiday-makers turning up. I can tell Julie needs a night off, too. She will be cooking for the guests five nights out of the seven that they are here. It's very hard work.

We stand together and wave to each writer as they leave; all smiling, and all promising to come back.

"Thank God that's over," Julie says, and I laugh. I take her arm and we walk back into the heart of our little world, where we will have a cup of tea and a chat for a while, or sit quietly and listen to the birds; look admiringly at our gardens and hanging baskets, or out towards the line of trees; drinking it all in and letting the week which has just been wash over us.

7

It is amazing how easily and quickly change takes place at Amethi. From pretty much every waking moment being about the writing course, we have now already welcomed our new guests for the week and thoughts of the writers have almost flown my mind. As always, there are a couple of things which stick with me; mostly, Tony's story. His words dredged up some of those feelings about Geoff and have brought them closer to the surface when usually I try to keep them tucked away; aware and accepting that they are there but no longer allowing them to colour how I see the world, and myself. I've been thinking about how Tony was after he'd read out loud. Aside from appearing to enjoy Colin's story, I thought he was quiet and withdrawn over lunch. When we were all saying our goodbyes, amidst lots of hugs and promises to keep in touch, visit again, meet up, etc. Tony barely spoke to me, which I found disappointing as I thought we'd got on well.

Luckily, some counterbalance was found with Helen, who was on a high after her successful reading. I can still see her face now, grinning as she drove away. She had decided to stay down in Cornwall for a couple of extra days, determined to write a little more; "I know it sounds cheesy, or pretentious, but this place is so inspirational. I feel like I could write forever."

"I know exactly what you mean." I spoke to Bea and got Helen a room at the Sail Loft. "You'll have the second-best chef in Cornwall there," I said, thinking of Jonathan and realising I should have invited him to lunch on Sunday, too. He's been quite down since Lydia broke things off; it's been over a year now but he can't seem to get over it. Sometimes I can't believe he's the same cocky young chef of four years ago.

Whereas before any residual feelings from guests – positive or negative – would have lingered and become more predominant when I returned home to my own company, now I have Sam to sound off to.

He knows all about Geoff, of course, and when I explain about Tony, Sam told me what I already know. Hearing somebody else say it was incredibly helpful: "You weren't to blame. You weren't responsible for Geoff. I know you know that, but I can imagine it's harder to feel it. But you weren't. I only met him that one time, but remember what he did… he didn't tell you I'd been to see you. And you spent the next ten years with no idea what had happened to me. I don't mean to make this about me – I just need you to remember why you ended your relationship with him."

These last words were the most helpful as they brought back to me how manipulative Geoff was, and controlling. It doesn't mean I am glad he died but I was reminded what a troubled soul he must have always been. I don't know why. Was it just him, or had something happened to him that shaped his personality, and ultimately the course of his life?

"I'm going to run you a bath," Sam said, "and you can wash away the week while I make us dinner and open a bottle of wine."

"That sounds pretty perfect," I smiled and kissed him

slowly. "We can celebrate one week of living together."

"I feel like we've hardly seen each other. I can't believe it's been a week already!"

"I know. Let's make the most of tonight, and even when the new guests are here, it won't be like this week. The residentials take up all my time and energy."

"I love seeing you doing it all, though," Sam said. "It suits you. And I've got to say, it's kind of sexy, you being in charge."

"Oh really?"

"Really."

"Maybe the bath can wait a while. I know another way to take your mind off things."

By the time Sunday lunch has come around, I already have plenty of new concerns to take over from my memories of the writing course. There are four different sets of guests this week, one of which is a group of friends from uni, all celebrating turning forty this year. They want me to organise a night out clubbing and while we do have a couple of small clubs in town, I think they want something bigger so I'm finding out what is going on this week and looking into logistics. Part of me thinks, *You lazy buggers, you could do all this yourselves*, but it is part of our selling point that we will manage events and bookings for guests; acting in a way as holiday reps – although I am definitely not going clubbing with them. Actually, I'm feeling pretty pleased with myself as I've discovered a proper beach party up in Carlyon Bay, which has been developed commercially. I think it will fit the bill for my guests, although it's not exactly Ibiza.

Luke is picking Sam and me up to take us to Sunday lunch. He has to drive up to London later today so won't be drinking. We are ready early and sitting in the sun in the car park, holding hands. It's a still day, and incredibly dry. The grass is yellowing but the wildflower meadow is going strong despite the drought. I watch a pair of small, blue-winged butterflies chase each other past us, dancing through the air. I squeeze Sam's fingers gently and kiss him on the cheek.

"What was that for?"

"Just... this. It feels perfect."

"It does, doesn't it?"

"I'd kind of like to just stay here with you today, but it's going to be so good to see everybody together, and show off my new live-in partner."

"I have met them before, you know."

"Yes, but you were just my boyfriend then. Your status has improved considerably."

"Let's go show off, then," he laughs, hearing a car turn in. Luke, the flash bugger, has the roof of his convertible down. The sunlight glints off the sharp edges of his car. Julie is waving madly from the passenger seat.

"Look at you two, you power couple," I laugh, kissing Luke on the cheek as he gets out of the car.

"You know me. Never happy unless I'm showing off," he smiles, pulling the seat forward and letting me into the back. I slide over behind Julie and squeeze her shoulder. "Alright, mate?"

"Yes! And also under strict instructions from Luke that there is to be no work talk. That's why he's put the roof down, so we can't hear each other on the way to the Cross Section."

"Sounds very sensible," says Sam, joining me on the back seat.

Luke clicks the seat forward, climbs in, and we are off.

The car speeds along the narrow lanes and away towards the estuary. I sit back and hold Sam's hand, thinking of Kate's advice to try to be in the moment. My stomach flips with happiness and I think of the four of us; Sam and Luke, Julie and me, meeting when we were teenagers. Who would ever have thought that we would be in the position we are now? I close my eyes, feeling the sun on my face and the wind from the open-topped journey on my skin. Life is good.

We are the first to arrive at the restaurant. I did manage to ask Jonathan to come, too, and it feels like I will have all the people here who I care about most; in Cornwall, and beyond.

Mum and Dad get here soon after and pretty much bypass me, making a beeline for Sam instead. The son they never had, I always tease them.

"How are you, Sam?" Dad says, pumping his hand up and down.

"Let go of him, Phil," Mum says, giving Sam a kiss on the check.

"Come to make an honest woman out of our girl?"

"Dad!" I exclaim.

"Phil!" Mum says, whispering into his ear.

"Oh, no, sorry, I didn't mean you two should be getting married. I just meant, now you're living together, I..."

"It's OK, Phil. Don't sweat it," Sam says, grinning. "Come on, let's go and get some drinks."

He shepherds Dad towards the bar and I sit down next to Mum.

"So..." she says.

"So."

"All going well?"

"Yes!" I grin. "Really well. I can't believe it, Mum. I mean, actually I've hardly seen him all week but it's just so good, knowing he's going to be there when I get in. Even if I am just falling into bed every night."

"And his new job starts tomorrow?"

"Yes, which is a good thing. Oh, and Sophie's going to be doing some work experience with him."

"Well, that is lovely. It will be really good for both of them."

"It will," I smile, as Dad approaches with a tray of drinks. Sam has spotted Kate, Isaac and Sophie and gone to greet them. Sophie hangs off his arm as they walk over to the table.

Slowly, the others arrive. Next come Bea and Bob. Then Jonathan, alone – I hope he doesn't mind, stuck here with all these couples, not to mention his boss. He smiles warmly, though.

"Thanks for inviting me, Alice, it's really kind of you."

"It's not kind at all; you're part of the fam, bro."

"Don't try and do street talk."

"Sorry," I look mock-ashamed and give him a hug. "How's the Sail Loft?"

"Same as ever!"

"And life outside the Sail Loft?"

"Also the same as ever."

"Met anybody… interesting?"

"No," he says, "but I'm not looking. You know that."

When he first came to work with me, Jonathan was a bit of a ladies' man; then Lydia came along and – I hate this expression but I am going to use it anyway – tamed him. Now she's graduated and found a job in London and decided to start life there single. I don't blame her. She is only twenty-two and before she went to uni she was helping to support her family; working with us at the hotel while she completed her studies. Now she's achieved so much, and has so much ambition, I can see that she doesn't want to be in a relationship, much less one which will have her travelling for hours at a time to spend the weekend here. Still, I am sad for Jonathan.

He had suggested to her that he got a job in London, but that wasn't really what she wanted, either. And he's a Cornish lad – and making a great reputation for himself down here. He has his sights set on opening his own restaurant in two years' time. Sometimes I wonder if it's right to let ambition get in the way of love but who knows? All any of us can do is try to make the right decisions in life. Nobody knows how it's going to turn out.

I sit between Mum and Bea; there is no seating plan, we all just settle quite naturally, with the minimum of fuss. There are still three empty seats.

"Who ever would have thought my brother would be the one that kept everyone waiting?" Bea smiled.

"I know! But I guess he's got a good reason."

Tyler came along when he was eighteen months old; a little over a year ago, and far sooner than David and Martin had been expecting. He is a little red-haired bundle of energy, who has turned their lives upside down. Suddenly, they are late to events (like today) or cancelling or rearranging things at the last moment. I wouldn't say that they are neurotic, but they definitely let the smaller things get to them.

"It's just such a huge responsibility," Martin has said to me, more than once. "I mean, it's the best thing ever, but I hadn't anticipated quite how it feels to be accountable for this little person's life, or education, or health. At least he can speak and tell us if and where he's feeling bad. Imagine if you had to look after an actual baby!"

I know very little of Tyler's background; David and Martin decided that they wanted to draw a veil over it. "Not because we don't trust you," David explained, "but we just want you to get to know Tyler as our son. He hasn't had the best of starts but we're going to reset the clock now."

Whatever they are doing, it seems to be working; even if they are late for everything these days. They have been fortunate to be able to both work part-time so they are practising a true sharing of responsibilities. Which is not to say they don't also have their fair share of arguments about fatherhood.

"I'll call him," Bea says now, but there is no need as I see three figures approaching the door.

Other diners look and smile at Tyler, who is incredibly cute in appearance. *Wait till he's been running round your table shrieking for five minutes*, I think. He is definitely what they call a handful at the moment but he is only two-and-a-half years old. And I have never seen David look happier.

"Bea-bea!" Tyler shrieks now and runs across to his auntie, who pushes her chair back, pulls him onto her lap and wraps her arms around him, covering him in kisses until he wriggles and giggles, pushing away from her.

"Hello, young man," I say, and he grins at me, flinging his warm little arms around me. "And hello, dads," I look up at David and Martin, who both look exhausted.

"Hello, Alice," Martin smiles and pulls a seat back. David sits two seats away, the spare chair for Tyler in the hope that between them they can keep him occupied for at least part of lunch.

"So in the words of Gary Barlow, you're back for good,

63

Sam?" David grins at my beautiful boyfriend.

"I am," Sam smiles. "How's life, David?"

"I have never been so exhausted. Never! Aren't they meant to sleep through by this age?" He does look tired but the proud look he is casting towards Tyler tells a different story.

"Ha!" says Mum. "I hate to tell you this but Alice didn't sleep through till she was eight. Remember, Phil?"

"Oh yeah, I remember alright. Opening your eyes to see a little ghost girl standing about five inches away from your face."

"*Muuuummmmm*," my darling mother mimicks. "*Can I sleep in your bed?*"

"Alright," I say, "that's enough of that. And probably not what David and Martin need to hear right now. Thank you. Let's concentrate on what we want to eat, shall we? And you can stop grinning at me like that, Sam."

Tyler has a small fish and chips, and milk served in a mini milk bottle, with a striped paper straw in it. I watch Martin help him squirt ketchup onto his plate, and can't help but smile at the enthusiasm with which the little boy tucks into his lunch, inadvertently coating his face with ketchup – although I don't suppose he'd much care if he knew.

Not yet, I think – *but one day*. I know I want that one day. However, the reality of what David and Martin are enduring is enough to tell me there is no rush. As soon as he's had enough food, Tyler starts wriggling, wanting to get down, to run around.

"Can't I just finish my lunch?" David wails.

"I'll take him outside," Sophie says. "We can go out on the decking, can't we? Have a look at the sea." I see Sam's proud look.

"Oh, I don't know…" David says. "What if…"

Martin reaches across and puts a hand on his husband's. "It will be fine. If you're sure you don't mind, Sophie?

"Not at all," she smiles and I watch her take Tyler's hand and walk across to the double doors with him, chatting all the way.

David visibly relaxes. "You've got a wonderful daughter there," he looks at Kate and Sam, who are sitting next to each other.

"I know," Kate says, and it looks like her eyes are brimming with tears. I hope she's OK. "Actually, we have something to tell you all, don't we Isaac?"

Isaac, by nature a very quiet and unassuming man – until you get him in front of a yoga class, when he takes no prisoners, smiles and nods. "We do."

I suddenly know what's coming. I look at Sam.

"We're having a baby," says Kate, to a round of congratulations.

"No wonder you've been glowing! I thought that was just a turn of phrase," I say, "but it's actually true, isn't it?"

"I don't know about that," she says modestly.

"I guess Sophie knows?" Julie asks.

"Yes, of course. She's… well, actually, I'm not quite sure how she is about it. She hasn't said a lot has she, Isaac?"

I turn to look at Sophie, who is busy crouching down with Isaac and looking through the gaps of the wooden balcony, looking towards the water below. I suspect she will make a brilliant big sister.

"It's quite an age gap," Isaac muses.

"She'll adapt," says Mum. "It will all feel very normal, very quickly, I'm sure."

I know that Mum had a miscarriage when I was about eight years old. That she and Dad had tried for years to have another baby but it just didn't work for them. I don't really know how that felt, or if it still bothers her now. I move almost imperceptibly towards her, feeling the warmth from her.

"I hope so," Kate smiles, "because we're over the moon." She looks it.

"You might be glowing but you don't look pregnant at all," I say. It is hard to imagine Kate's body has ever borne a child; she is so incredibly toned.

"No, she only started showing at about seven months with Sophie," Sam says, and I feel a very rare twinge of jealousy, or possessiveness, that he was there for that vital stage of Kate's life. It quickly passes.

"I'm older now," Kate says, "I am quite sure I'll be the size of a bus soon."

Somehow, I doubt it.

"Congratulations!" Luke says. "This calls for champagne, for those of us who can – for me, and for Kate I guess, it's lemonade."

"I'll stick to water, thanks Luke," says Isaac. He smiles around at all of us. "I don't drink much anyway but while Kate's pregnant I'm going to be living like I am as well."

He looks so earnest I can't help but smile and I can well imagine what my dad is thinking. He likes Isaac but finds him "a bit too new age."

"That's so good, Isaac," Bea says. "I salute you."

We murmur our agreement while Luke smiles at a nearby waiter and orders enough drinks and glasses for all. Sam goes to fetch Sophie and Tyler, who does not want to come in. Sam hoists the little boy onto his shoulders, crouching low as he comes back through the double doors into the restaurant, and the little boy is soon giggling.

We toast the excellent news, then Luke insists that we

toast Sam's return to Cornwall, and we sit a little longer, chatting and drinking coffee, before beginning to disperse, making our way back into the Cornish sunshine, a glorious Sunday afternoon stretching ahead of us.

8

Back at Amethi, Sam and I decide to have an afternoon snooze. It's so hot again today, we put a fan on the chair in the corner of the room and close the curtains but open the windows wide. In a small room like this, it gets very hot very quickly; and now that there are two of us to share the space, it feels like it is more stifling than ever.

We strip to our underwear and lie side by side, just the backs of our hands touching. Even that is slightly uncomfortable after a while, the sweat prickling my skin and sticking the pair of us together. Although if there is one person I wouldn't mind being stuck to, it's Sam. I hear the slightly angry buzz of a wasp, which must be just by the window. *Don't come in*, I think, exhausted now that dinner is over and I have a couple of drinks inside me. I could do without a game of Put the Wasp Out.

"That's some news about Kate," I say.

"Hmmm? Yeah," Sam says sleepily, eyes closed and lips curled into a small smile.

"You already knew," I realise.

"Yeah, well, Sophie told me. You know what she's like. It just slipped out the other day. Which is good because it means she's excited about it. But Kate doesn't know she told me, so I had to be surprised today."

I smile at the thought of Sophie letting the cat out of the bag. "How do you feel about it?" I watch Sam's face as I ask this question. His eyes remain closed, his smile stays put.

"I think it's great, as long as Sophie's OK with it. There's going to be quite an age gap there," he opens his eyes, "but that's just the way things are. If you and I…"

"Yes?"

"Well… I know we haven't talked all that much about it but if you and I decided to have children, they would be much younger than Sophie, wouldn't they?"

"I guess." I know full well they would be. And I don't know why I am trying to sound like I haven't thought all of this through already. Sam's right; having been preoccupied with getting through the long distance phase, not to mention his studies and my life being taken over by Amethi, it is not something we have talked about a lot but it's definitely crossed my mind, more than once. A lot more than once. I note that he said 'they' – meaning children, plural. I like that idea.

I can't imagine it right now, though. How would everything work? Amethi is going brilliantly, but what if Julie or I – or both of us – had kids? I think of the little enough spare time I have as things are; imagine having a baby strapped to me as I do the rounds of the place, or sleeping in a Moses basket by my desk while I take bookings, plan courses, order flowers and the million and one things that need to be done to keep this place running. The baby is usually asleep in my imaginings. Babies sleep a lot, right?

"It's not strange for you, with it being Kate..?" I press.

"What? No, of course not. I'm happy for her. And Isaac's a good bloke, despite those weird green smoothies he makes. And putting pressure on the rest of us. Living like he's pregnant… what's he going to do? Strap a cushion to his stomach?"

"You can buy those fake pregnancy bellies, I think. And

69

actually, that's a great idea. If you and I ever do have children, I'll get you one of those while I'm pregnant."

I lean over to kiss him, feeling the soft curly hair of his chest brush my bare skin. I pull back slightly and smile at him, and we kiss again. He pulls me to him.

"We're meant to be sleeping," I say.

"Sleeping's for wimps."

Nevertheless, we do sleep; fitfully, in my case, but happily. I seem to keep catching myself just before I fall asleep properly; my mind awhirl as usual but this time with thoughts of children and my biological body clock, which people seem to witter on about a lot (not mine specifically, I should point out – just the general concept). I am thirty-two now so not old by any stretch of the imagination but in just three years any pregnancy I might have would be classed 'geriatric'.

It was Julie who told me this. "Unbelievable, isn't it?"

"Are you sure that's right?"

"Yes, because in pregnancy terms, I suppose that's how it works. You're moving towards the tail end of the years when you could have a baby."

"I definitely saw something about an Italian woman who was pregnant in her sixties."

"Yes, you idiot, you did, but I don't think that's exactly the norm."

"Imagine having a baby in your sixties."

"Imagine being in your sixties."

We had both laughed at this but I know it made me think and I am sure Julie was already thinking about it. She's told me before that Luke is really keen to have kids.

"I think it's since his mum died; but maybe that's wrong, perhaps he'd have been like this anyway. He's always on about his mate John in London, who's got three kids already – sometimes Luke stays with them when he's over that way, and he can't shut up about the kids when he gets back."

I had smiled at this, thinking it fitted completely with Luke. I can imagine him as a dad, scooping up a giggling toddler and placing it easily onto his shoulders; it is less easy to imagine Julie as a mum, perhaps because I have known her so well, for so long, but maybe also because I know she has never been sure if she wants to have children or not.

"I remember you saying you hated the idea of being a mum, back when we were at college."

"Yeah, I did, didn't I?" she said thoughtfully. "What did I know back then, though? What did either of us know?"

"True."

This conversation plays back inside my mind now, then I think of Mum and how she talks about the years when I was little; trying to keep her career going but wanting to be with me. "I sometimes wish I'd just stopped work altogether, made the most of that time, because it flew by. And the guilt I felt, when most of the other mums were clearly full-time mothers. I felt like an outsider in the playground, at the end of a school day. It was clear that many of them had gone to baby and toddler groups together and formed these bonds. I always felt like they were looking disapprovingly at me, but now I wonder if that was more to do with how I felt about myself."

Mum had worked part-time after I was born, until the time I was about nine, when she went back full-time. My grandma – Dad's mum – had looked after me when Mum was at work and I know she had been quite a force in encouraging Mum to carry on with her career. Grandma died some years ago but I still miss her. She was ahead of her time in her outlook on life; especially the role of women in society and the world in general. Mum has said to me more than once that Grandma knew the other mums better than she did; but Grandma was proud of her daughter-in-law and I know she talked about Mum's achievements – often too loudly for my liking – in the playground at the end of the school day, or at the park. I suspect some of the other mothers may have felt unhappy that they weren't working. It seems it's hard to win in this situation: work, and you're not being a good enough mother – don't work, and you are not making the most of yourself, or earning an income; you are sustaining the 'man's world' model.

"I don't think I missed out on anything, Mum," I nudged her teasingly but she looked genuinely regretful.

"I swore that if I had another baby, I'd take more time out to do it properly."

"You did do it properly with me!" I exclaimed indignantly.

"I know, but the guilt… you have no idea."

"Look at you now, though. And throughout my childhood – you are a brilliant role model, and a brilliant mum."

She had hugged me and smiled, as though I was being kind, but I meant every word of it.

Sam is breathing deeply next to me but I eventually accept that I am not going to be able to sleep right now. I decide to let him have the room; to remove my own body heat from the scenario and hopefully help him keep cooler that way. I move into the bathroom and turn on the shower.

The water is a welcome relief. In the winter I like my showers so hot that Sam always complains if he gets in after me. In the summer, I like them just warm enough that I don't shriek when I step under the needle-like water. I tried a very, very cold shower but ended up with a sharp, acute headache.

Staying under the flow for quite a while, I turn the temperature up a little, as my body cools and my skin complains, in the shape of goose pimples. I hum to myself and lather my body with the shower gel I've bought from the health food shop in town. The tea tree oil makes my eyes sting and clears my mind. I wash my hair with lemon grass shampoo, and eventually I step out of the cubicle, turning the rush of water off, and wrap myself in a towel.

When I moved in here, Julie bought me a set of soft, fluffy towels, the same red as the tiles on the kitchen floor; knowing that I would no longer be able to steal hers. It makes me smile every time I use one, although this is sometimes tinged with just a hint of sadness at that stage of our lives being over. I did love living with her.

Padding downstairs, I find a basket of clean clothes, which I really should have unpacked and put away, and I put on a thin, sleeveless dress and some clean underwear (not in that order). Can I really already be sweating? I feel like this is the hottest it has been all summer. It's humid, in fact.

Somewhere outside, there are children laughing and I smile as I always do at the thought of the guests; the holiday-makers. It is quite special to make a living from something which is purely about making sure people have a good time. The whole point of Amethi is to make people happy.

I open the top half of the stable door into the hallway, the smell of a barbecue drifting lazily across the still air. Despite my huge lunch of falafels and various salads, finished by a clotted cream ice cream, my stomach stirs. I can hear adults' voices, too; laughing gently. The pop of a cork from a bottle.

Remembering family holidays from when I was little, I walk through to the kitchen, the tiles soothing my hot feet. Rummaging in the fridge, I find some cheese and some chilli jam, and a jar of pickled onions. There are crackers in the cupboard, and some apples on the side. I pour a pint of sparkling water from the bottle in the fridge. The glass immediately breaks into a sweat. Setting it all on a tray, I slip on some sandals and go out through the back door, into the secluded garden. I like to have privacy from guests and I am sure they feel the same the other way.

For a while, I sit and just think, letting the day and the week, and everything, wash over me. The tame little robin flits down, loitering just far enough from my feet to be able to make a hasty exit if necessary. Gently, I crumble a little of the edge of a cracker and scatter the fragments. The bird flinches, moves back a short distance, then seeing that I mean no harm hops forward, pecking up the crumbs. My secret dream is for some of the birds at Amethi to become so tame that they land on my hands. I don't tell anybody else about this because it will make me sound like I'm nine years old. The robin and I eat in comfortable silence, both keeping one eye on the other, although for different reasons.

The cheese makes me thirsty and it isn't long before I've finished my glass of water. I go inside to get another, this time picking up my tablet. I go to the bottom of the stairs, listening for signs of life in the bedroom, but all is quiet. I should wake Sam soon, or else it's going to be night-time and he'll wake up in the morning, feeling unprepared for his first day in his new job. I will just have another fifteen minutes, though.

When I go back outside, I startle a small gang of

sparrows, who seem to have replaced the robin. They rise up rapidly, twittering to each other, and they are gone. I notice the sky is darkening over the line of trees but here the sun is still in full force, and I am glad for the shade of the cottage. Logging on to the tablet, I scroll through Facebook for a while. Seeing nothing interesting, I move on to TripRecommends.co.uk. It looks like we have a couple of new reviews.

The first makes me smile widely. Good old Colin:

Five out of five cartwheels
Colin Haygarth
Superb location, wonderful hosts, and incomparable writing tutors.
I had the pleasure of attending a writing course at Amethi and I can hand-on-heart say I would love to return for another. In a secluded location not far from the Cornish coast, you can practically feel the sea from Amethi but you don't have the hustle and bustle (and queues of traffic) of the nearby town. The peace and solitude make it an ideal place to write, while the hosts – Alice and Julie – are so welcoming and lovely that it is a perfect place to stay. While I was there to write (and I should mention that the tutors were second-to-none), I can imagine many a happy holiday at this beautiful place. Julie's cooking is fantastic, too. Restaurant-quality but in the comfort of a home setting. Cannot recommend highly enough.

As I read this through for a second time, there is a sharp crack of thunder in the distance. I look up to see the darkness enveloping more of the sky over towards the coast. I scroll down to the second new review. It is anonymous and when my eyes take in the wording, I feel my stomach drop and my heart starts beating more quickly.

Two out of five cartwheels
Anonymous
Not all it's cracked up to be
Although in one of the most beautiful parts of the country, and penned as a luxury holiday experience, Amethi has many areas ripe for improvement. When we arrived, the kitchen was not clean – crumbs on the work surfaces and dirt on the floor. The bedroom was furnished very sparsely and the bed linen clearly old and well-used. The hosts were nice enough but very young and this showed in the standard of care received.

Wow. I haven't seen a bad review before, and I have to say I don't like it. I read it three more times, looking for clues as to who has left it. It doesn't say the dates that this review relates to so it's impossible to know but the first people who spring to mind are Sheila and Ann, neither of whom were reluctant to criticise other places they have stayed previously. But there is no mention of the writing course, so perhaps it wasn't them.

Could the kitchen have been dirty? I wonder. And the floors? I highly doubt it. Cindy has extremely high standards, and I always do a walk-around before guests arrive, as a quality control measure.

It's just a bad review, I reason. *People leave them for all sorts of things. We were bound to have one at some point.* And the overwhelming impression people will get is positive; thirty-nine brilliant reviews to one poor one. Nevertheless, reading those words was like a kick in the guts.

The darkening of the sky creeping ever nearer, I gather my things and go inside. I put the tablet on the counter and switch the kettle on. Busy myself with tidying up. There are crumbs on the work surface, and dirt on the floor. I wipe the surface down, and sweep the floor, the words of the reviewer gnawing away at me.

I refrain from texting Julie. I don't want to ruin her evening off, and besides, she always tells me I'm obsessed with reviews. Well, it's been true so far as they've all been amazing. And I know what Sam will say if I tell him. Exactly what I've told myself. It's one review; one reviewer. Maybe they complain about everything. Perhaps they're having a hard time and just taking it out on other people in whatever way they can. But this place is more than my livelihood; it's my life, and I know Julie feels the same way.

I glare at the tablet, and go to the front door. As I do, there is flash of lightning, illuminating the whole sky. I hear the shriek of children, and the voice of one of the adults telling them to go straight inside. "Mummy and I will just clear this lot up, and be in right after you."

The smell of the barbecue has gone, and I feel like the air is crackling. While I have longed for something to break the back of this heat, there is a small part of me that craves its intensity and the way it makes me feel like I am in another country.

In rolls the thunder, heavy and hard, cracking the dark sky open and setting free the rain, which falls mercilessly, soaking everything in its path.

9

"It's just a review," Sam says when I tell him, moments after waking him. I have brought him a cup of tea, and a bagel filled with cream cheese and slices of cucumber from Amethi's vegetable garden. I didn't mean to blurt it out but the words fell straight from my mouth, as soon as he looked alert enough to hear them. "Thank you," he says, blinking as he takes the plate from me and I place his mug on the bedside table.

And it is just a review, I agree with him. Just a review. From one person.

But who? I try to push the thought from my mind; enjoy the evening with Sam. This is our night off before the madness begins once more, and twofold seeing as he is starting his new job tomorrow.

"Is it raining?" he asks.

"What? Oh, yeah. I can't believe that storm didn't wake you up."

"It feels different; I almost feel cold."

"I know." I open our curtains so Sam can see the deluge, then I close the window. The raindrops rattle angrily against the glass. Amethi looks like it has pulled on a disguise; or revealed its true identity. From sun-soaked haven to stormy and angry. I wish that I could paint because I'd love to create a picture of the place as it is right now. The sky heavy with brooding clouds and all of the gravel turned dark in the downpour, tiny puddles already

78

pooling here and there.

It may not be holiday-making weather; and it's certainly not an evening for sitting outside, but I love it. There is something about being at the mercy of the weather which feels thrilling; when there is so much that as humans we have harnessed control of, this is something we can do nothing about.

I have been at Amethi through two winters now and it can definitely feel bleak here, but there is a pleasure to be gained from that bleakness and always, if you look close enough, there are some small details which add brightness – and which may not have been there were it not for the bleakness.

The foxes, for example, slinking along through the wildflower meadows (which in the winter are really just meadows). They may not feel so at ease in a busier place. I know they've set up home in the line of trees but I barely see them during the busier, summer months. And the birds seem more confident in winter; in fact, I think I have more chance of success in achieving my dream of making them semi-tame in the winter months. They will come closer to me then; maybe hunger is driving them but I like to think it's because of the calm of this place.

Because it is incredibly calm. The thing which I value perhaps above all is the quiet. On a cold January day, when the world – or at least this part of it – is nursing a month-long hangover, Amethi is not open to guests and the absolute peace of this place is overwhelming. Perhaps to a different person it could appear lonely, but to me it is absolute bliss. Julie and I work part of the month; it's a chance to get everything in order, but we also close for two weeks, to make sure that we get a proper break. This winter just gone, Julie and Luke jetted off to the

Caribbean. I was going to get a last-minute break in the sunshine but I stepped outside one morning, into a white-clouded day, the ground cracking with frost and a light layer of mist just skimming the top of the meadows. I stood for a moment, and then a moment more. Breathing deeply. Listening carefully, but hearing nothing. I realised I just wanted to stay put. And I wanted time to myself; untouched by anybody else, like a new layer of snow.

I told Julie what I was doing and while I think part of her thought I was mad, she also seemed to get it. "Alice, you do whatever you want. You need a break, and you shall have one, however you choose to spend it."

Sam knew as well, of course, but to everybody else – including my parents – I had gone on holiday. I felt slightly guilty but as soon as I hit the supermarket, stocking up for my 'week away' this feeling was replaced by a sense of excitement. A week off. A whole week at home. To myself. I couldn't remember the last time I'd had a lie-in; I would normally wake early even if I did have a rare morning off.

I piled my trolley with all sorts of unhealthy food; almond croissants and tiger bread; huge chunks of cheese, bars of chocolate and bags of crisps. I topped it up with salad and fruit, and bottles of sparkling water – to dilute the effect of the red wine I'd also slipped into the trolley.

Back home, I set myself up with a free trial of Netflix, and another of Amazon Prime.

"What about your car?" asked Julie.

"What about it?"

"Well what if, say, your dad happened to come up here. Just to check that everything's OK while you're away."

I smiled. Julie knew my parents well. That was just the kind of thing Dad would do. I felt a twinge of guilt at lying to him… *Not telling the truth*, I unconvincingly told myself, as if there was a difference.

"Let's move it to the far end," Julie said. "We can hide it behind the shed. Cover it with some of that old sacking. You'll need to keep the curtains closed on that side of your house as well; otherwise anyone coming to the car park will see that there's somebody at home. And you can't have a fire – the smoke will be a dead giveaway."

"You seem to be enjoying this," I laughed. "Maybe you were made for subterfuge."

"I think I'm just living vicariously through you. I mean, I love the Caribbean, and having some time with Luke, of course. But a week to myself… and at Amethi… sounds like heaven."

This made me feel slightly better. I had worried that I would regret not taking the opportunity to get properly away. Staying put turned out to be an excellent decision.

The first day, I woke up early. I shrugged, and just wriggled down the bed a little, enjoying the feel of the clean bedding and the weight of the duvet on me. And the quiet. I had breakfast downstairs, chose a film to watch on Netflix, and I just lay on the settee, in my pyjamas, a throw over me for warmth. Despite Julie's excellent advice, however, I decided that I would just have to take my chances when it came to the fire. It was worth the risk.

I built the fire and made myself some lunch, after which I promptly fell asleep; the combination of the warmth from the dancing flames, and a stomach full of food, and the knowledge that I had NOTHING TO DO all worked their magic. When I woke, I felt deliciously guilty. An illicit afternoon sleep; only it wasn't illicit. I was on holiday. I let myself relax that week and did not once regret my decision to stay at home.

In a strange way, the rain is a relief. It is a reason to stay indoors. I love the weather we've been having, and the long, light nights – but I always have a feeling I need to be making the most of it all. To have the weather dictating our evening's activities – Sam and I just move downstairs and watch a film – means I can't feel guilty, or as if I am missing out. I even forget about that stupid review, although I am vaguely aware of a niggling annoyance somewhere in my mind.

We drink a glass of wine each, and eat pistachio ice cream from the tub. After the film has finished, Sam goes into the kitchen and prepares his lunch for the next day.

"Are you nervous?" I ask, following him in.

"About making lunch? No, I've done it a few times now."

"Very amusing. No, about your new job."

"I suppose I am, a bit. I know I worked there before but then I knew it was for a specific amount of time, and that I'd be going back to uni at the end of it. Now, it feels like I need to put everything into it. And there's a small worry that I won't enjoy it as much as I've always hoped."

"I know what you mean," I put my arms around his waist, and lay my face against his back, feeling his warmth and his strength, "but you know you're going to be brilliant. I know it, anyway." This line of work has been Sam's dream, for at least as long as I've known him, dating back to when we were eighteen and, I suspect, a long time before that.

"Well thank you," he turns to me, kissing me gently and slowly and I take my time, to be in the moment. Hear his breath, and feel the soft smoothness of his lips against the bristle on his chin. I slide my arms up so that my hands cross paths behind his neck, and our bodies press closer together.

A sharp flash of lightning outside and the lights go out.

"No!" I say.

"No!" groans Sam.

We both know what this means.

The thunder is throwing its weight about when we go outside, coated in waterproofs from head to toe. We run through the rain, Sam pulling me along; despite our annoyance at being interrupted – what was that I was saying about not being able to control nature? Maybe not such a great thing after all – we are giggling.

"Is everything OK?" Mrs George is standing torch in hand in the open doorway to her holiday let.

"Yes, just got to get the generator going. So sorry. This does happen very occasionally," I say quickly, breathing fast. "But don't worry, we'll have it up and running again very soon."

And we do. It's easy enough to get the generator going – but very noisy – and when we retrace our path across between the buildings, Mrs George waves to us. "Thank you! What a nightmare!"

"One of the perils of living in the sticks," I grin. "I'm sorry for the inconvenience."

"No problem," she says, and her husband sticks his head round the doorframe. "Thanks, guys. Hope you're not too wet."

"We're fine! Are you enjoying your stay? Sorry about the weather!"

"Not much you can do about that," he grins.

"Hopefully it will revert to wall-to-wall sunshine tomorrow."

"Fingers crossed."

We wish each other a goodnight and Sam and I head back to our cottage. While the waterproofs have kept the vast majority of rain out, as I peel them off I feel sticky and sweaty.

"Fancy a bath?" I ask Sam.

"Just me – or the two of us?"

"I thought the two of us. Unless you want to be alone."

"Oh no, I think I can cope with sharing with you."

"You finish getting your stuff sorted for tomorrow and I'll get it ready."

I pull the bathroom window nearly shut, and dim the lights so that they look like stars twinkling in the ceiling. With the taps running on full, soon the room is hazy with steam. I add a few drops of essential oil to the water.

"It's ready!" I call, quickly stripping off in the bedroom and dashing back to the bath, sliding into its hot embrace just as I hear Sam's footsteps on the stairs.

"That looks incredibly inviting," he says.

"Come in and close the door; keep that steam in here."

"I'm sure we can make it steamy ourselves."

"Smooth," I grin.

"It was a bit cheesy, wasn't it?" Sam is standing on one leg, pulling off his clothes.

"But your method of undressing is so seductive, it makes up for it."

"I'm tempted to throw this at you," he says, pulling a sock off his foot.

"That would definitely ruin the atmosphere," I smile, close my eyes, and sink my head under the water momentarily. I can hear the pipes settling down after their efforts, and a kind of weird echoey noise.

I come up to find Sam fully naked. "This is like having a bath with a mermaid," he says, pushing the hair out of my face and kissing me before climbing in. He leans back, his legs going to the outer sides of the bath while I slip mine in

84

between them.

"Aaaahhhhhh." I feel like I can see his muscles relax. He closes his eyes and I look at him in the dim light. I am reminded of the time he came to me, after Luke's mum died. It was another stormy night, and we shared a bath then. I remember the utter despondency on his face as he sat alone amid the bubbles, asked me to join him. It's hard to believe what a long way we have come.

Eventually, we go to bed, and go to sleep. I have put a towel on my pillow to stop my wet hair soaking it through. I can't be bothered to use the hairdryer, even though I know I'll regret this laziness in the morning. Sam is out like a light, his breathing deep and peaceful. I lie for a while on my back, his arm around me. The rain seems to have stopped now and our bedroom window is open to the night. The room is dark, the air steeped with quiet. An occasional owl breaks the silence but other than that, all is still.

10

"It's just a review," says Julie, although she looks quite annoyed by it.

"Should we respond to it?" TripRecommends.co.uk gives the business owner the opportunity to reply to any comments. In my head, I've composed a variety of responses but I am not sure which approach – if any – is best.

"I don't know," says Julie. "Maybe we should ask Bea. She'll know the right way to do this."

"Good idea, I'll give her a ring in a bit."

I read the review again.

Two out of five cartwheels
Anonymous
Not all it's cracked up to be
Although in one of the most beautiful parts of the country, and penned as a luxury holiday experience, Amethi has many areas ripe for improvement. When we arrived, the kitchen was not clean – crumbs on the work surfaces and dirt on the floor. The bedroom was furnished very sparsely and the bed linen clearly old and well-used. The hosts were nice enough but very young and this showed in the standard of care received.

The cheek of it. I don't know if I am more offended by the comments about the cleanliness, which must be an outright lie (why would anybody feel the need to lie about it?) or about Julie's and my age. Our rating is now 4.4 so has just dropped below the 'excellent' bracket into 'superior'. Not the end of the world, but it is still rankling with me.

"You can reply," says Bea, "in a very diplomatic way. But sometimes I feel like in responding you are breathing life into the review. I don't know. Maybe it's better to ignore it. You have plenty of brilliant feedback and scores – overwhelmingly so."

"But it's so annoying – and not even true," I whine.

"I bet you've spent ages thinking about what you'd like to say to them."

"Of course."

"Well, what I sometimes do is type out a few of the things I would like to say – but I don't post them. That way you can vent all your anger but when it comes to an actual response, if you really want to give one, you can tone it down. A calm and reasoned response will reflect well on you. An angry and emotional one won't – and might give credence to her claim that you are too young to be in this game."

"But…"

"I know!" she laughs. "Of course you're not. But when people are looking at online reviews, the words and the pictures are all they have to go on. They can't meet you, or Julie – or know what Amethi is like. It is a very flat experience and sadly people sometimes like to cause trouble or be negative, for whatever reason. Try not to let it get to you; maybe just a line or two like 'We are very sorry to hear you weren't 100% happy with your stay at Amethi. We can assure you that our standards of cleanliness are extremely high, and we refresh our supplies of bed linen every year'. Don't make reference to the personal comments; your response can show people that you are mature."

"That is great advice, thank you Bea!"

I feel much better for speaking to her. When I was managing the Sail Loft we did get poor reviews, of course, and they did annoy me, but it feels so much more personal here at Amethi. I type out almost word-for-word what Bea suggested, run it past Julie, post it and resolve to put the whole thing behind me.

Sam set off early for work this morning. He felt full of nervous tension, and excitement.

"Good luck," I smiled as I kissed him. "Not that you'll need it."

"Thank you," he said, giving me a perfunctory kiss back, his mind elsewhere. I felt anxious on his behalf as I watched him drive away. This is his lifelong dream, come to fruition; the result of four years of study, too, which nearly drove a stake through the heart of our relationship. I watched until the car has vanished through the curtain of trees before going back into the office.

Although it feels cooler outside since last night's storm, the office is still clinging possessively to its own heat. I push the window open a little further, enjoy a whisper of breeze against my cheeks.

Typing my password into the computer, I refrain from checking out the TripRecommends site and instead busy myself reviewing our bookings over the next few months; identifying any gaps which I might have to offer at a reduced price.

The phone goes; a family wanting a break in the last week of the school holidays. I take their details and deposit payment, and one such gap closes. August is now fully booked.

In September we have another yoga retreat. I wonder if Kate is going to be able to do it. And another booked in for November. Knowing her, she'll still be performing downward dogs and planks when she's in labour. I try to imagine her svelte body reshaped to accommodate a growing baby.

Sophie seemed excited about the whole thing when I spoke to her at the restaurant. "But if it gets really noisy, can I come and stay with you and Dad?"

"Of course you can," I put my arm around her shoulder. "And you know now your dad's back, you can come and stay with us whenever. There's a spare room with your name on it. But that's something for your mum and dad to sort out," I added hastily, thinking perhaps I was stepping out of line.

"Maybe I can come for a couple of days a week and then every other weekend?" Sophie asked brightly.

"Well, erm, you can… of course, you can, but…"

"What are you two chatting about?" Sam appeared behind us, laying his arms lightly around our shoulders.

"I was just asking Alice what days I can come to yours? Now you're back, I mean, you and Mum can have joint custody."

"Sophie," Sam had laughed, "you can come to us whenever. You know that."

"But it might be good to know what days. It's what Josh does with his mum and dad."

"And who, might I ask, is Josh?" Sam raised his eyebrows while Sophie blushed.

"A boy in my class."

"And are his parents as cool as yours?"

"Dad! You're not cool!" Sophie grinned.

"Well said," I put in.

"No ganging up on me, you two." Sam took his arm away from me and placed his hands lightly on his daughter's shoulders. "Soph, you can come and stay any time. Isn't that right, Alice?"

I agreed, happily.

"Your mate Josh, well maybe he's got a different set-up; perhaps his parents had to work out a plan like that when they split up, to fit in with their lives, and make sure that they both get to see him as much as possible. If you really want to set specific days then we can do but I don't think we need to. Do you want me to talk to Kate about it?"

"Erm, I don't know," Sophie's little nose wrinkled. I studied her face, thinking how much older she looks now than when we first met, and yet how still she can take on the look of a much younger girl. It's like her teenage and child selves are battling each other, only I know there is no way that the child is going to win.

I decide to send her an email, which she thinks is quaint and old-fashioned, her lines of communication with her friends being entirely through instant messaging.

Dear Sophie,

It was great to see you yesterday and your dad is really excited to be back in Cornwall with you again.

He has gone off to his new job this morning and can't wait for you to be able to join him on your work experience.

I was wondering if you'd like to help me decorate the spare room a little; so that when you come here it doesn't feel like you're in a spare

room but your own space. Would that be a good idea? If you'd like to, let me know and we can go shopping one day, if that's OK with your mum and dad of course.
Love Alice xxx

I press 'send' and almost simultaneously, a new email lands in my inbox. The computer alerts me with a beep.

Sheila Donoghue. One of my prime suspects for the bad review. This should be interesting.

Dear Alice and Julie,
    I just had to write to tell you what a wonderful week I had at Amethi, which is a magical place. You two should be very proud of yourselves.
    Vanessa and Rosie were inimitable tutors and I have returned home feeling truly inspired and energised, and ready to write!
    I hope to book on for the same week next year, and I will be telling my friends and family about this lovely place to stay. I will also, of course, write you a glowing review online.
    By the way, on the shelf in the shared area, I left you a signed copy of my first volume of poetry; I don't expect you to read it, of course, but it's just a little gesture of my appreciation.
With very best wishes for now,
    Sheila.

I am stumped. Who'd have thought that Sheila – the woman who seemed to spend all week criticising and patronising, would be so full of praise? My mind begins whirring. Maybe this is a ruse; she's written this to us so that we won't suspect her of leaving that review. But, thinking about it, she wouldn't be the type of person to hide behind anonymity. No, if she was behind it I imagine she would probably have signed off with her full name and the titles of her books, and details of where you can buy them. Then a thought hits me, about the book she has left behind. What if it is her behind the bad review, and she's left some kind of clue in the book?

I race downstairs and around to the communal area, unlocking the door and going straight in. Sheila's book is turned outwards so it's the first one to catch the eye. Of course.

I pluck it from the shelf and turn the slim volume over in my hand. *Scenes from a Life*. It has a beautiful cover; a copy of an oil painting, similar in style to L.S. Lowry. Opening it up, I see that the artwork is attributed to herself. She is a genuinely talented lady. She has also inscribed the front page;

To A and J, with memories of a wonderful week. S.

The S is signed with a flourish – large and curling. I turn a couple more pages and I begin to read. What I find within is not what I would have expected of Sheila at all. It would seem she is a dark horse. But then, I remember her short story. It's very easy to judge people, and often unjustly, I reprimand myself.

I feel foolish when I think that I have just run down here; what was I expecting? I chastise myself again, for having let one bad review work me up so much that I think there might be something sinister going on. Sitting on one of the sofas, I open Sheila's book.

It begins with a short poem, about school days, and being the only girl without a pony or, as it transpires, a dad. I read on, finding beautiful words, revealing more surprises about Sheila, assuming that it is autobiographical. Growing up in a small town; achieving a scholarship to an all-girls school; picked on for her second-hand uniform; finding her mother passed out from drink.

No wonder she is happy now to tell the world about her gardener, and her swimming pool.

I slide a piece of paper in as a bookmark; I want to read more of this revealing book, but for now I must get back to work.

The day passes quickly, as days often do here, and I hear the guests coming and going. The Georges and their small children were out by the time I came into the office this morning but back in time for lunch. Not that I keep tabs on the guests' comings and goings; I just happened to hear the kids running around outside. Their laughter echoed around the walls of the buildings, making me smile.

In the early afternoon, when I popped back home for a sandwich, I saw Mrs George sitting outside, reading a book.

"Hi," I said, not really wanting to disturb her.

"Hello," she semi-whispered, and grinned. "Sorry! It's just they're all having a nap – including David. This is a very rare occurrence, getting a few minutes all to myself. And it's so beautiful here, and so quiet."

"I'll leave you to it, I can imagine times like this are to be treasured. Can I get you a coffee or tea or anything?"

"Oh no, I... actually, do you know what? Yes please,

that would be really lovely. Please can I have a cup of tea?"

"Of course."

I trot home, putting the kettle on while I make a sandwich. I make a pot of tea for Mrs George; put it on a tray, alongside a cup, saucer and a small plate of biscuits. I take it out to her, not wanting to consider whether I am going the extra mile as a reaction to the TripRecommends review.

"Oh wow!" she smiles widely. "That is so lovely of you."

"It's my pleasure. Enjoy! If you wouldn't mind leaving the tray and crockery out afterwards, I'll take it back – it's from my own kitchen."

"Well, in that case, that is extra lovely of you. Thank you so much."

I head back home and eat my sandwich in the back garden, washing it down with a glass of water. I have to consciously make myself relax sometimes; not rush straight back to work. So I sit, for a few minutes, letting my food digest and looking for the robin but in the mid-day heat it is nowhere to be seen.

Back in the office, tucked between the usual business emails, I see a message from a familiar name: Anthony Burrows. This is Tony, who was here last week.

Dear Alice,
I wanted to let you know how much I enjoyed last week and what a perfect place Amethi is for writing. I feel refreshed and inspired.
Please also thank Julie for the amazing food.
I am sure we'll be in touch again.
With best regards,
Tony

I am feeling much better now, about that one review, and I know I have over-reacted. The feedback from Tony, Colin and Sheila has been very positive. I send a quick message back to Tony and a longer reply to Sheila, telling her how much I admire her poetry, and the cover artwork. I don't want to sound gushing but credit where credit is due, and I am still feeling slightly bad that I suspected her to be our mystery mean reviewer. Then I switch off the email altogether, for a while, so that I have no distractions while I go over our plans for the next few months. I must speak to Kate at some point about her work here. Both autumn courses are fully booked so I hope that she is able to do them, but I really don't know how she will feel when she's pregnant. In fact, I think, I should grab the bull by the horns now. I pick up the phone.

"Hi Kate, it's Alice."

"Hi, Alice! I was going to ring to thank you for organising lunch yesterday. That was lovely."

"It was really good to have everybody together," I smile. "And I wanted to say again congratulations about your pregnancy."

"Thank you! We're so excited. But I guess you're ringing about work?" I can hear a smile in Kate's voice.

"I… yes, I am. I'm sorry. I would rather just be excited for you, but I was thinking I'd better ask you about it now, while I've got some time to make any changes if necessary."

"No need to apologise, I promise. I've made commitments to you and Julie, and I'm not going to let you down. I've already got somebody in mind to take over my classes when I get too big, and I've mentioned the Amethi weeks to her. I still want to do them myself, but I was thinking that Lizzie could come with me, and we could

95

run the courses between us. She can do the demonstrations if I'm not able to pull off all the poses. And I'm still up for planning some courses for next year; Isaac and I are going to share all the parenting."

I am grinning as I listen to all of this. I should have known that Kate wouldn't let us down and I love the fact that she has already come up with a way around it all. Julie and I will have to meet Lizzie but I am sure Kate wouldn't be looking to hand her classes on to somebody unsuitable.

"Well that all sounds excellent," I beam. "And I really am sorry to have to ask you about work stuff right now."

"Don't be! It's your livelihood – and mine! We businesswomen have to stick together."

My mind casts back to a night out Kate and I had, when I barely knew her, and she took me around the nightspots in town. A slimy creep who had sailed into town on his expensive boat had tried it on with her but she had properly put him in his place. It seems she's turned this determination into something more positive now and I feel a glowing pride for her, and Julie and me – all relatively young women, running our own businesses and doing what we love. Luck plays a part in it, for sure, but none of this would have happened if we hadn't made it.

"Thank you, I really appreciate it. Maybe you can bring Lizzie up here for one of the morning sessions, in a week or two. Do you think she'd be up for that?"

"I'm sure she will."

"Brill. Give my love to Sophie, and Isaac. See you soon, Kate."

"And give mine to Sam."

A couple of years ago, I would never have dreamed that we would have such a modern, grown-up relationship.

When Sam gets back from work, I am waiting for him, leaning on the wall of the car park. I left Julie plating up the dinners, and offered to help her deliver them but she insisted I come and greet Sam.

"It's his first day in his new job! You need to be the supportive wife."

"Except we're not married."

"You may as well be."

"Well, OK… I suppose if you put it like that."

"Oh, I forgot to mention I made dinner for you two as well."

"You…? Julie, that is so lovely of you. Thank you so much."

"Well, you deserve it and so does Sam. It's nothing fancy."

"Oh. I was hoping it would be."

"You ungrateful bugger! I'll bring it over to yours once I've got the guests sorted out."

I hugged her. "Thank you, you wonderful human being."

"No problem. Now don't forget his pipe and slippers."

"Ha."

I can see from Sam's expression as he drives into the car park that he's had a good day. He sees me waiting and his face breaks into a huge smile. My heart leaps. The sun is glinting off the assembled vehicles and it's a beautifully warm evening, without any of the humidity of the previous weeks. The ground is bone-dry, as though last night's storm never took place.

Sam comes over and kisses me.

"Good day, darling?" I take his hand.

"Fantastic. How about yours?"

"Yeah, pretty good," I admit. "And I got some lovely

97

feedback from some of last week's writers."

"There you go, people love it here," he squeezes my hand. "You knew that really, though."

"I want to hear about your new job. This place is old news now. Come on, Julie's made us dinner."

Hand-in-hand through the sunshine and birdsong, we walk home together.

11

There's another bad review. And a tweet, although I don't find this until later.

The review comes after the week's visitors have left, just as I am checking things over for the new tranche of guests. Like the first review, it is anonymous:

One out of five cartwheels
Anonymous
Won't be coming back!!!!!!
We booked this as a luxury holiday. I don't know how the hosts define 'luxury' but I don't think I would agree with them.

While the food was very good, I was disappointed with the standard of accommodation and the 'grounds' as they are described on the website. Fields of long grass and weeds; dark, muddy woods; gravelled paths and parking area. There was nowhere to sit outside.

In addition to this, there were a number of unanswered queries, which I had put to the manager, who seemed to take no notice.

As my headline says, I will not be coming back!!!!!

The over-use of exclamation marks aside, this is a well-put-together bad review and I am flummoxed by it. Who can it be from? Surely not one of the guests who has just left? The Georges came to say thank you and their children had drawn a picture of me and Julie with a great big 'Thank you' scrawled in crayon. The other guests seemed equally happy, all smiling graciously as they handed over their keys, and promising to come back. Mr Jenkins did say he'd leave a review but I did get the impression he meant a good one. What if he didn't? What if this was his experience of Amethi?

Our rating has dropped to 4.2.

I can feel my heart beating ten to the dozen and, clutching my phone, I sit on the bed, which I really shouldn't, as it's a guest bed and has been made up perfectly by Cindy. I'm meant to be doing my final checks before the new guests arrive. I should not have looked at that website. I feel deflated.

I've always thought this was the most perfect place to come and stay. It's quiet, and secluded, and to my eyes entirely beautiful. Perhaps I'm mistaken. Maybe this is to my taste, and Julie's, but we've got it wrong.

No, I reason, we have had loads of fantastic reviews and return visitors already. Yet, despite all the lovely emails of thanks we have received when people return home, and the recommendations to friends and family, it's these two measly, unpleasant reviews that resonate with me. It's a terrible tendency of people in general to focus in on the negative even when it is outweighed overwhelmingly by positives. One criticism will stand out amongst twenty compliments and become a focal point. I am aware of this but find it difficult to think any differently.

Sam is out for the day, with Sophie, and I'm not going to interrupt them; besides, I already know what Sam will say: ignore it, it's just one bad review. The only problem is, it's not just one. Not when it's put alongside the other one. There are two now, and they might back each other up. I know Julie is less disposed to think in such a way so I stand up, straighten the bed covers, lift my chin high, and go to find my friend.

"Julie," I say gently to her hunched-over back. I can see that something is wrong. This is confirmed when she doesn't turn around. "It's not… the review, is it?"

She sniffles. Oh no. Maybe it is. Perhaps I am not blowing this out of proportion, if Julie's taken it so badly.

"No, Alice, it's not the review. We were bound to get a bad one at some point."

Ah. So she hasn't seen this second one. No surprise, really, as it was only posted an hour or two ago, and Julie is nowhere near as obsessed with reviews as I am. What, then, is the problem? I place a hand lightly on her back.

"Stop chopping for a sec, and tell me what's up."

She turns and I see her eyes are red. "It's just the onion," she says, and we both laugh. She is chopping peppers.

"Come on, what's up? This is definitely not like you."

"Oh, it's just hormones. I got my period this morning."

"OK." I let this explanation settle between us. Julie does not normally suffer from period pains or major mood swings. "And you didn't want to get your period? Is that it?"

Her eyes meet mine. "Yes."

"Julie! You're trying for a baby?"

"Well, yes, kind of. We decided to just see how things go."

"Bloody hell!" My mind is working fast, taking it in.

"I'm sorry I didn't tell you before. I just, I know it sounds silly, but I didn't want to acknowledge it to anyone because

101

I have no idea when or even if it is going to happen. Maybe I can't have children. Maybe Luke can't. We don't know. And I didn't want you to think I was going to abandon you with Amethi. That is never going to happen. But ever since we stopped using any contraception, I've started to really want this."

"Oh, Julie," I say, pulling her into an embrace. "I would never think you were going to abandon me. And it's really exciting that you want to be a mum. And it will be the most beautiful baby in the world." I wonder if I am saying the right thing; Julie is right, she doesn't know if it's going to happen, so it feels a bit flippant to be talking about a child that we don't know will ever exist.

She sobs into my shoulder for a moment then I feel her physically pull herself together and back. "Thanks, mate," she snivels, wiping her eyes and her nose with a tissue. "I feel like a right idiot. I'm sure it's coming off the pill, it's sending me all over the place."

"Well, don't they say it can take a while to get back to normal after you stop taking it? This is probably your body playing about with your emotions! Bloody hormones. Look, why don't you just stop for a few minutes and come and sit outside in the sunshine? I'll bring you a coffee, or whatever you want," I add quickly, wondering if she's going to be off caffeine and alcohol now she's trying to get pregnant. "You don't get to enjoy this place nearly as much as I do, so get out there and take a few minutes to let it work its magic."

I won't take no for an answer, and practically frogmarch my friend outside. She laughs. "Coffee would be great, please. I'm not at that point just yet."

Busying myself in the kitchen, I let it all sink in. It is no surprise that somebody our age is thinking of starting a family. I always used to think, though, that of the two of us it would be me who settled down first; Julie, although a bit of a serial relationship-hopper, was always a bit more fly-by-night. I was the steady (boring) one, with a dependable job, my own flat, paying into a pension and taking it as read that I would settle down and have a family one day. But life rarely runs as we might expect it to.

I carry a tray laden with coffee, warm milk, and crumbly Cornish shortbread outside. Julie is sitting in the sunshine, eyes closed like a cat. She looks happier now. Her eyes squint open when she hears my footsteps on the gravel.

"Sorry about that," she smiles.

"Don't be! You must know by now that you don't have to apologise to me, and I'm really glad you told me what's going on."

"It's not that I didn't want to, but – and this sounds silly, in fact it sounds like something you'd say—"

"Thanks very much," I grin and she returns the smile.

"—it felt like I was jinxing things by telling anybody. Saying the words out loud. How silly is that?"

"It's not silly," I say and she snorts. "OK, maybe a little bit."

"And then Kate pipes up with her pregnancy, and it made me think maybe it was my turn, too. And whenever I see David and Martin with Tyler, it makes me want it really badly. I know, I never thought I'd be the maternal type. Turns out I really am."

"You will make a brilliant mum," I say. "I know, I know, it may not happen. But it's early days, Julie. Sometimes it takes months to get pregnant. Years, even; sorry, that's not helpful, is it?" Since when was I the worldly-wise one on this subject, anyway? I am hardly qualified to talk about it. There's a little part of me that wishes it was Sam and me,

103

though, trying for a baby. But we're not there yet. We've only been living together for two weeks, for one thing. That does seem a little bit hasty. And besides, we really, truly do need to enjoy some time together, just the two of us, now we have finally got to this point.

"Thank you, Alice," Julie tops up her coffee with some warm milk, stirs in a tiny spoonful of sugar. "I think you're right about coming off the pill. I'm feeling much better already."

"Good," I smile and take the milk from her, pouring some into my cup. "And now we're sitting out here, together, enjoying this beautiful place of ours."

"This is totally lush," Julie sighs. "We don't do it enough. We should make sure we do it, at least once a week."

"We definitely should," I agree but we both know that, despite all good intentions, it will never happen.

***

Julie's situation is not a welcome distraction, but a distraction nevertheless. Back in the office, however, I find that the gnawing sensation returns and I go back to TripRecommends.co.uk.

I can see there is another new review. My heart starts pounding, even though I tell myself it's silly.

5 out of 5 cartwheels

My heart slows. I sigh audibly.

The George Family

God bless them.

Will DEFINITELY be coming back!!!!

Like the previous (anonymous) reviewer, we too booked this as a luxury holiday. It was a real treat for us, as we have a young family. I don't know what some people define as 'luxury' but to us it was the spotlessly clean accommodation; the beautiful location – wildflower meadows, to anybody who knows anything; a small wooded area where the kids could play; very well-tended and neat pathways and parking area. Not to mention the delicious food cooked for us and brought to us in the comfort of our own home. As anybody with small children will know, they can be very fussy – and often you will end up cooking different meals for everybody. At Amethi, all this pressure is taken away from you and Alice and Julie could not have been more accommodating.

All of our queries were answered promptly and there were some beautifully personal touches. My wife particularly appreciated having an unexpected afternoon tea brought to her while the rest of us enjoyed a nap.

I can't promise you afternoon tea; that is not on the menu, but it is an example of the thoughtfulness of the people who run Amethi.

As my headline says, we will be coming back!!!!!

I laugh out loud. If Mr George was here now, I would hug him. This comes right underneath this morning's review, and I can't believe he's gone to the trouble of answering all of the points made criticising us.

Nevertheless, as the time approaches for our new tranche of guests to arrive, I start to feel on edge. What if they've seen that horrible review, and last week's? What will they be expecting when they get here?

I make myself busy, reviewing the costs of the previous month. The phone rings.

"Hello. Amethi," I say, circling back to my sales training at World of Stationery, and smiling as I speak. *They can hear you smile*, the disembodied voice of the trainer whispers in my mind.

"Oh yes, hello there," comes a slightly gruff male voice. "This is Mr Sampson, I've booked a week with you at, erm… Ameethee, is it?"

"Oh yes," I say, dredging through my internal booking system to see if the name rings a bell.

"Yes, well, erm, I'm sorry to say we would like to cancel."

"Oh. OK, I'm sorry to hear that. Would you like to rebook for a different week instead?"

"No, no, that won't be necessary."

"That's fine." Alarm bells are ringing in my mind. "You do know we can't refund your initial deposit?"

"I do, thank you. Sorry."

He hangs up, leaving me rifling through the online system to find him.

Mr Sampson. October 25th for one week.

This booking only came in two weeks ago, while the writing retreat was taking place. So he has only paid that initial £50 deposit; the second part – equalling half the price of the stay - was due before the end of this month.

Paul suggested that we do it this way, saying that giving people the retainer option might get people to book more easily as they wouldn't feel like they were having to pay so much up front. "You ask them to make it up to 50% of their stay before a month is out, then the remaining 50%

needs to be paid a month before the holiday takes place. This should weed out the time-wasters, and will give you enough time to rebook if necessary." This strategy has worked well so far and we have had very few full cancellations; generally, people want to rebook.

How has Mr Sampson changed his mind so quickly? I did think at the time that it was a bit odd for a single man to want to come and stay during half-term week. I even joked with him about it but he said he wanted to get to Cornwall before winter began and there was some event or other going on that week, as well. So it does seem a bit odd that he's cancelled so abruptly, and without any explanation. I can't help but think – again – of the poor feedback people will be reading if they check us out online. Thank god for people like the Georges; but then it's a case of who potential guests believe – and whether they would want to chance their precious holiday, not to mention their money, on a place which might not live up to expectations.

I mark Mr Sampson's week as free once more and cast my eye over the booking system, clicking through the next few months. It is always a comfort to see how far ahead we have bookings for, and that they far outnumber the free spaces.

The first of the new guests are due soon. Cindy and I have put milk and butter in their fridges; emptied vases of their previous week's inhabitants, tipping the contents – including the green, sludgy water – onto Amethi's vast compost heap; stocked the welcome hampers with cookies, fudge, teabags, local honey and marmalade, and a loaf of bread fresh from the bakers' this morning, the smell of which will greet the newcomers as they walk into their home for the week.

I go to click on TripRecommends.co.uk but stop myself.

Instead, I scroll across the browser tabs; I have far too many open, as usual. I check and close each one in turn and then I come to Twitter. I see we have a new mention.

Twitter is not something I use a lot. Julie tends to keep this side of things up. It's just not something I can get into. And, to be honest, I think it's better suited to individuals, who can join in chats and express opinions freely. Julie and I keep our opinions – of which there are many – out of all things business, aside from things like supporting environmental measures and showing our commitment to making Amethi as eco-friendly as possible.

I refresh the screen and immediately wish I hadn't.

@CornwallLover1242
Recent stay at @AmethiLuxury absolutely appalling. Don't buy all this #ecofriendly rubbish. Not sure what they were burning but smelled like tyres or something. Probably local farmers pay them to get rid of waste. Handsome enough place but piles of rubbish everywhere. #ripoff

What the…? This is out-and-out bullshit. I quickly click on CornwallLover1242's profile. Joined Twitter ten days ago. Eight followers. Following 367 – all Cornwall-, tourism- or environment-related. This can only be targeted at Julie and me. But who? And why?? My breath is short as I read and reread the tweet. What do I do? Should I respond? Will that only make me look guilty?

There is no time to decide now, as I hear the familiar crunch of gravel, and a car slowly travelling up the drive. The first of this week's guests are here.

12

"This does sound pretty suspicious," Sam says in the evening, coming to lie next to me on the bed. I have been here for a good hour or so, lying on my back, watching a small cobweb in a top corner of the room sway gently to and fro with the slightest movement of air.

"But you have to put it in perspective, it's just one tweet – and two bad reviews, and they are not necessarily linked."

"But if they're not linked then there are people out here who hate Amethi!" I wail, aware that I am sounding like a child. Sam treats me accordingly, putting his arm around me and stroking my shoulder consolingly.

"On that point—" he sounds irritated, and probably rightly so, "—those two reviewers on TripRecommends don't say they 'hate' Amethi."

"Well they don't like it," I sniff, maintaining my childishness. An image of Kate springs through my mind *– Now come back into Child's Pose and relax for a minute*. Kate! Could it be? I very, very quickly disabuse myself of that idea. I've been there before, thinking she was sabotaging Sam's and my relationship, only to discover it had been Sophie. That is all water under the bridge now and besides, Kate has no reason to hate me anymore. But that is what this feels like. Hate. And I know it seems over-dramatic and that Sam is being reasonable, as he should be, but I have a terrible feeling in my stomach.

109

It's why I'm inside on a beautiful summer evening, rather than out in the sunshine. I don't feel like I can face the guests now. I managed the usual greeting and settling everybody in, then told Julie I had a headache and she said I should come and have a rest, she'd take the reins for the rest of the evening.

I've heard her coming and going, bringing the meals across to the holiday-makers, and I heard her and Sam greet each other before he got to our house. It all sounded so cheerful. It made me feel even more miserable.

"No," he sighs, "apparently not, but you have just also had some glowing testimonials, so on balance you're actually doing better than worse."

"I guess."

"Look, I'm starving, I'm going to get dinner started. Why don't you have a shower and freshen up – wash all this away – and then come down? It's Saturday night. You have a day off, or the closest thing to a day off, tomorrow. And I'd like us to have a nice weekend. It's back to work for me on Monday."

"Sounds like a good idea." I sit up, determined to pull myself together. "I'm sorry. I haven't even asked you about your day. How's Soph?"

"She's great."

"I know that!" I smile. "Did you have fun?"

"Yeah, we just went down the coast, had a bit of beach time. She reckons she's getting pretty good at surfing so I said I'd take her next week, on Saturday. If you don't mind?"

"Of course not! You should see Sophie whenever. I just love knowing that you're coming home to me at the end of the day." A feeling of happiness engulfs me, all thoughts of stupid reviews and tweets banished.

I feel much better for having Sam back, and making myself think about him, and Sophie. I definitely have a tendency to let things get out of proportion in my mind if I spend too much time alone.

I sing to myself in the shower, thinking of Sam downstairs. By the time I'm out of the bathroom, leaving a cloud of peach-smelling steam behind me, there is a delicious aroma of spices wafting up the stairs. My stomach rumbles and I realise I missed lunch today. I pull on a t-shirt and cut-off denim shorts, pulling a hoodie over my head and actually glad that I feel the need to. Respite from the stickiness of last few weeks.

Sam is singing to himself in the kitchen and I watch him from the doorway for a moment; see the way that his shoulder blades and the curve of his back make his t-shirt hang just so, and his low-slung jeans sit on his hips. He has let his hair grow a little longer, and keeps saying he must get a haircut but I like the way the extra length makes it curl.

I sneak up behind him, snake my arms around his waist. He jumps.

"When did you come in?"

"Oh, I've just been spying on you from the doorway for a while."

"Have you now?" He gives the pan a shake, tossing some sweet-smelling peppers in the air, and turns around.

"Yep," I smile up at him. "And I liked what I saw."

"Now you sound like an old perv."

I laugh. "Maybe I am."

"Well, I quite like what I see, as well." He kisses me lingeringly. "But I am cooking, and I'm at a crucial stage, so you're just going to have to control your urges and pour out some of that wine."

"I am sure your accent's coming back more strongly," I say, doing as I'm told.

"Is ee?"

"You must be reacclimatising to your homeland."

"Arr. Maybe you're right, moi babber."

"Would you prefer some cider?"

"Typical upcountry girl, coming down here with your preconceived notions."

"They must come from somewhere."

"I'll have you know we speak the Queen's most excellent English, thank you very much. And isn't Prince Charles the Duke of Cornwall?"

"Yep, and he's a bumpkin as well."

"Right. That's it!"

I back away and dodge out of the door before the flying tea towel has a chance to reach me.

***

Despite having fallen asleep easily, I wake in the early hours of the morning – before the day has had a chance to come to life – and immediately think of that stupid tweet, and the horrible reviews. It takes all my self-control not to find my phone and look again. What if there was something new out there?

It's only a tweet, I tell myself. And probably nobody's seen it. I don't really get Twitter. My few forays on it have resulted in an occasional Like or Retweet but generally speaking, my messages seem to go into the ether, mingling with all the other pointless, inane words which people have put out there. In amongst them all might be cries for help; or maybe the fact we're relying on some social media system which governs how many characters we can use is a cry for help in itself, from all of us.

'Handsome enough place'. Sounds kind of Cornish. I think of the mugs in one of the shops in town which say 'Drink up, my 'ansom'.

So is it somebody local who's sent it? I sigh. I can't think of anybody I've really annoyed but then perhaps I've done something without being aware of it.

Those TripRecommends reviews – I can cope with them, just about, although they seem greatly unfair. But this is an out-and-out lie, and it makes me worry that there will be more to come. Are all three messages linked? From the same person? Or just incredibly bad timing. Or perhaps CornwallLover1242 has seen them and decided they want a piece of it. I've read and heard a lot about trolling online but I don't know how we've managed to attract the attention of somebody who enjoys this kind of pastime. I imagine a hairy troll sitting under a bridge, tapping away at his phone, chuckling at the ingenuity of his latest nastiness.

Various responses to all three things roll around my mind, but I know I won't post them. I know enough about modern-day public relations to not feed the troll, if this is really what this is.

I sigh again, and lie in the darkness, comforted by Sam's presence but still unable to get back to sleep. The owl hoots in our line of trees; our protection here from the outside world. In the middle-of-the-night loneliness, it feels like the protection has been breached.

I'll feel better in the morning, I tell myself. Thing always seem much worse in the middle of the night. Sam snores a little, rolling onto his back. I kiss his bare shoulder, move against him so that I can feel his warmth against my side. It's dead still out there and I strain my hearing to see if I can hear the sea. I think I can but more likely it's my mind playing tricks on me. Nevertheless, the thought of it soothes me.

I take long, deep breaths. Use some of Kate's tricks to relax. Clench all of my muscles up as tight as I can and then let them go, feeling my body sink into the mattress. Alternate nostril breathing is another one. But I can't let go of the thoughts about those messages. The nastiness. A single tear squeezes from my left eye, rolls down the side of my face and onto the pillow. I imagine it in detail, seen under a microscope, the tiny beads of moisture creating a small damp spot.

The owl calls again.

I am in for a long night.

13

"There's another one, Alice," Julie says reluctantly from the door of the office.

"What?" I turn around, my eyes grateful for the break from the spreadsheet they've been glued to for the last forty minutes. It takes me a moment to realise what she's talking about and then I know.

"On Facebook this time, on one of the Cornwall groups. Bea just rang to let us know."

I'd heard the phone go but Julie had picked it up on the kitchen extension before I'd had a chance to tear myself away from the rows and columns of figures – income and expenditure, broken down to the smallest of details. I should show this to anybody who thinks we've just fallen on our feet.

"Here," Julie gently pushes my wheeled chair aside slightly so that she can get to my keyboard. She presses 'save' on Excel and minimises the spreadsheet then opens a browser window, opening Facebook on my profile. "It's this one."

The 'Adore Cornwall' group has been set up by holiday-makers fed up with the abuse they received on some of the more authentic Cornish Facebook groups. Tourists (emmets) would be baited by locals looking to get a rise. Cowardly and irritating and guaranteed to get a result, every time. A splinter group formed 'Adore Cornwall' (subheading: 'ignore the Cornish') as a private group and it now has upwards of sixteen thousand members. Both Julie and I have joined, as have lots of local people who work in hospitality. This kind of group is a great place for free advertising of last-minute deals and vacancies due to cancellations.

I see the post Julie means immediately, as it displays a photo of Amethi. But something isn't quite right about it, and it takes me a moment to work out what. It's our place alright, but there seems to be a plume of black smoke billowing across the buildings and the otherwise clear blue sky, and a pile of what looks like tyres in the car park. Just like that tweet said. Closer inspection reveals a rusty-looking water trough and bins brimming with rubbish.

"Shit," I breathe.

"I know."

I look at the profile picture of the originator of the post. Jeff Halford. There is a photo which is clearly a stock image, of a man wearing sunglasses, laughing and revealing unreasonably white teeth.

The name resonates, being similar to that of Geoff, my ex – he was Geoff Hillford. I shudder. Look closer, at the words below the image.

This is so-called 'eco-friendly' Amethi, run by co-owners Alice Griffiths and Julie. Their website states 'while not claiming to be perfect we do what we can to reduce, reuse and recycle'. I beg to differ. They also claim to be family-friendly but my wife and I could not let the kids out of the house when we were there – see the smoke, the rubbish and the old rusty farm equipment.

"He's never stayed here," I say, "or at least not with that name."

"No, we've never had a Jeff Halford. Sounds a bit like…"

"I know," I cut her off. "Just something else to be weirded out about. But that can only be a coincidence. Have you looked at his profile?"

"I've tried, but it's locked. Looks like it was only set up a couple of weeks back, though – you can see when he joined and the other stupid profile pics that he's tried out."

Below the image are fifty-seven emojis of people's reactions: most are the 'angry face' with a couple of 'shocked' and one laughing.

"Fifty-seven people have seen this!" I say.

"At least," says Julie. "And there are comments," she reveals reluctantly.

I scroll down. There are eighteen comments.

This is disgustin. They say they eco-friendly it doesn't look like it. Won't be stayin there.

What are they burning? Looks rank. I wouldn't want to take my kids somewhere like that.

Just looked at the website myself. This is meant to be a luxury self-catering complex. Just what is this people's definition of luxury?

Putting aside any judgement towards the use of the English language, I immediately see how damaging this could be for us. I also notice that 'Jeff' has responded to the last comment:

I know. The one plus point was the food, which was excellent but I don't know why the chef has tied herself to this place.

I feel like I have been punched in the stomach. This is damaging for both Julie and me, but it's clear that whoever this is – and I am sure now that there is just one person behind all the negativity – has got a problem with me. It is not a good feeling.

"They hate me," I whisper.

"No, don't, I don't think that's necessarily…" Julie's words trail off, because she knows as well as I do that there's not much she can say. "Who the fuck is doing this?" she says angrily.

"I don't know. And what can we do about it?"

"I've already contacted the group admin to ask to have it removed."

"That could take ages," I say. "And look, it's been shared eleven times. This is not good, Julie."

"No," she sighs, "it's not." She falls back onto her own chair, using her feet to scoot across the room to me. "And I know, they do seem to have a problem with you. Which is ridiculous. If I knew who it was, I'd go and sort them out but I have got no idea who might be pissed off with you. You're not a pissing-off sort of person. If it was directed at me, I might understand it better."

I give her a small smile. "I've clearly done something, to somebody."

"Let's think," Julie says, putting her hand on my arm. "Let's get some coffee and go outside, let the place work its magic as you said to me the other day and get a bit of space to think in."

"OK." I really don't feel like it. What if some of our guests are around? What if they've seen that post? I feel ashamed.

"You hold your head high," Julie says. "You've done nothing wrong. And I've just responded to that post,

118

saying that the picture is clearly Photoshopped or something."

"But you're posting as yourself, it will link straight back to us."

"True. But it's his word – or hers, it might be a woman, you know – against ours. I typed out a long response, but realised it sounded like I was trying to dig ourselves out of a hole so I just said the photo was clearly not genuine, and put on a photo or two to prove it, and that people should come and see for themselves."

I pull my phone from my pocket, and open up Facebook. I click into the Adore Cornwall group. Three people have already 'Liked' Julie's comment, and I can see a response is already being typed out. I watch the dots appear and reappear. I realise I am holding my breath, wondering if this is going to turn out to be another comment from 'Jeff'. No – it's Angie George. I release my breath.

This is ridiculous. We stayed at Amethi just last week and it was fantastic. The kids loved it. My husband and I loved it. The management are just lovely – so welcoming and cannot do enough for you. The food is excellent and what a treat to be so looked after. I would DEFINITELY recommend Amethi to anybody and we will be staying there again. I would very much doubt that this photo is real. The place was spotless and very environmentally friendly. We were happy to let the children out to play in and around the buildings, and to take them into the little wooded area.

"I love the George family," I smile but I feel quite shaky.

"I think I'm going to stay off the coffee, it's only going to make me more nervy."

"Oh Alice, I'm sorry."

"It's not your fault. You're not Jeff, are you?" Another unconvincing smile from me.

"Ha! We'll sort it out. But let's try and work out who it could possibly be, shall we? Is there anybody you can think of?"

I rack my brains. "I really can't."

"No unrequited love interests?"

"No, nobody's shown an interest in me – except Sam, of course – since Paul."

"Well it wouldn't be Paul," Julie muses, "unless he's really good at double bluffing and has given us all this help just so he can knock us back down again."

"Seems unlikely."

"How about Shona?" she says suddenly. "You said she didn't seem that keen on you."

I think about Paul's girlfriend. I've only really met her a couple of times. She is in her early forties, tall and glamorous without looking like she's trying to be. Beautiful, glossy hair and stylish but understated clothes. Intelligent and successful, she seems perfect for Paul.

"Mmm, I don't know about that. I mean, she wasn't overly friendly but she seems pretty mature and I don't think Paul would be with somebody so petty."

"Yeah, but Paul wouldn't know, would he? And she is in London most of the time."

"Yes, but… no. No way. That seems ridiculous. She must know that nothing really happened between Paul and me. And she's met Sam."

"Don't underestimate how weird people can be," Julie says knowingly. "I mean, I hope it's not her. But let's keep her on our list of suspects."

"It's not much of a list," I say glumly.

"We'll work on it. We'll get to the bottom of it." She puts her arm around my shoulder.

"I know. Thanks, Julie. Look, I'm going to just get some water and get back to work. I need to sort out all those figures."

"And I guess I'd better get back into the kitchen. Dinner isn't going to cook itself."

I open the door to the steps up to the office, vaguely aware that I've barely acknowledged the beautiful sunshine the day has brought. My mind is fixed only on this situation, which seems to be going from bad to worse. A place like Amethi is built on its reputation. These posts and reviews carry a lot of power. The anonymity adds a sinister edge. I shiver slightly as I pass through the doorway, out of the light and into the shade.

14

As the week progresses, so does this campaign against us – or, possibly more correctly, against me. Because that is what it feels like.

There have been more posts from 'Jeff' on Facebook, in other local groups. Each time one pops up, we manage to get it removed – but usually it takes a little while to achieve this and in that time who knows how many people have seen them. Each post has a picture of Amethi, edited to be less than flattering, and whoever is doing this appears to be getting better at it. The additions to the images are more subtle – and he (or she) has ringed around them in red, as if to draw the viewer's attention, knowing that the details are not immediately obvious. The overflowing bins are a regular feature, and on one there is the image of an emaciated dog, tied up in the car park. This person is getting cleverer, and we are getting no nearer to finding out who it is.

We have three cancellations; not the end of the world, in the great scheme of things, and possibly incidental, but it feels like more than a coincidence. Each person has a plausible excuse lined up – illness, or a family wedding which has been arranged last minute – and of course I can't question them or it will seem like I'm accusing them of lying. It would begin to add credence to the image of me as a less-than-worthy manager and proprietor.

There has been only one new booking, as well, so the

schedule for the next few months is slightly more empty than it was before, and Julie and I are both reluctant to push any adverts out while this is going on.

"We need to get to the bottom of it, and nip it in the bud," Julie says.

"I know. And I feel really bad that you're being dragged into it."

"Don't be ridiculous! You have no reason to feel bad. It's not you doing this, it's some nutter with an axe to grind, for some unknown reason."

But I do feel bad – because the nature of the comments is always slanted towards me, either saying that 'the manager' had not responded to enquiries, or had made an incorrect booking so that when this person apparently turned up for their week's holiday, Amethi was full and the booking had been made for the week after. It's impossible to come back to any of these things without sounding like I am making excuses.

"But I keep thinking about you wanting to, you know, get pregnant." I don't know why I feel slightly awkward saying those words to Julie. I feel like I caught her in a moment of weakness, crying when she got her period, and no matter how well I know her, she will not have wanted me to see her like that. She doesn't say anything so I go on, "I know that stress is meant to make it harder to... conceive."

"Alice, my lovely friend, I'm not stressed. Well a little – but mostly on your behalf. This is a crappy situation but we will sort it out. I am more worried on your account; I know you're not yourself."

It's true. I feel horrible at the moment. Whatever I am doing, there is a hard knot at the bottom of my stomach; as if, even in the moments I am not consciously thinking about what has been going on, it's still gnawing away at me.

"You're being bullied, Alice," Julie says. "That is essentially what's going on. And I know I should say 'we' – because it's about our place, but I know if I was you I'd feel like it was being directed against me personally and I can imagine how it would make me feel. I can see how it's making you feel."

With Julie's kindly hand on my arm, I find tears welling up and I can't blink them away fast enough.

"It does feel like that. Like being bullied, I mean. And I think Sam is getting fed up. I mean, this is meant to be our honeymoon period. We are finally together, and he's just started his dream job, and everything's revolving around this… this shit."

"It doesn't have to," Julie soothes. "You need to try and take a step back, if you can. Look at the positives. All those people who have jumped to our defence."

This is true. We have seen an increase in positive reviews on TripRecommends; a result of a frank email from Julie to our previous clients, diplomatically suggesting that somebody has it in for us, and asking if people would be kind enough to post openly and honestly about their experiences staying with us. So many people have responded, saying how sorry they are that they had not left us reviews before now – *I completely intended to, but then I got home, and work got in the way … you know how it is.*

"And Sam is not fed up with you; he's worried about you. I am, too."

Oh no. The tears are flowing freely now. Julie pulls me to her and I lean gratefully into her shoulder, as she rubs my back and makes comforting shhh noises.

"You're going to be a great mum," I say, pulling back

and smiling sheepishly, wiping my nose and eyes on my sleeve.

"Here, take this," she says, handing over a packet of tissues. "I don't know about that – but I'd like to have the chance to find out."

"You will," I say, but instantly regret saying that. How can I possibly know? "Sorry – what I mean is, I really hope that you will."

"Thank you. I will definitely keep you informed. But that has to happen in its own time. For now, let's put an end to this nastiness. Have you had any more thoughts about who it could be?"

"No. None!" I exclaim self-pityingly, as though I am outraged that anybody could take a dislike to me.

"Then I think it's time to phone Paul."

"Paul? Really?"

"Yes. Really. I don't mean that I definitely think it's Shona, but she is one person with a reason to be unsettled by you. After all, it was you that turned Paul down. And she can see what a catch you are, even if you have no idea."

"Ha."

"I mean it. Now come on, go home and wash your face, straighten yourself out, and give Mr Winters a ring. I'll keep things covered here."

"Alice!" Paul's greeting is warm and friendly.

"Hi, Paul, how are you?"

"I'm very well. I'm just up in London, actually, planning to come back to Cornwall for the weekend."

"That sounds good," I say, wondering if I sound as stiff as I feel. "Are you with Shona?"

"Not at the moment, no, but she's coming back with me tonight. Did you want to speak to her?"

Paul's said a number of times before that I should speak to Shona about PR stuff. I somehow don't feel comfortable with the idea, and I'm not sure she'd welcome it.

"No, no, that's OK. It was you I was ringing to talk to. Do you have a few minutes?"

"Of course. Fire away."

The 'few minutes' become nearly an hour, as I tell Paul what's been going on and he checks out some of the posts and reviews on his laptop.

"What the..." he keeps saying. And, "Shit."

I lie back on the sofa and wait quietly, listening to him tapping away.

"This is horrible," he says. "You must be really upset. Do you know who it is? I mean, it must be just one person, mustn't it?"

"That's what we think." I explain to him how we are trying to get things taken down as soon as we see them.

"But people are sharing them and retweeting before you get the chance?"

"Sometimes, yes."

"Look at the lovely things you're having said about you as well, though. These outweigh the shitty ones."

"Yes, but there's no smoke without fire. Or that's what people will think."

"I'm not sure about that," Paul says. "Anyway, a rolling stone gathers no moss."

"And too many cooks spoil the broth."

"A stitch in time saves nine."

As I'm laughing, Sam comes in, looking at me quizzically, half-smiling.

"Paul," I mouth.

Sam looks like he's trying not to show any reaction at all to this. I know what he's thinking, even if he doesn't realise it. He backs out of the door and I hear his footsteps go up the stairs.

"Paul, Sam's just back. I'd better go and see him."

"Sure. Well, just keep me posted with all of this. And if you're about this weekend perhaps Shona and I can call by."

"I think it's going to be a busy one, I'm afraid. And I'm out on Sunday at David and Martin's."

"How are they getting on?"

"Oh, great, you know. Tired!"

"I can imagine," he chuckles. "I'd better go now as well, but don't forget to let me know if I can help at all. Or Shona."

"Thank you."

"And Alice?"

"Yes?"

"Take care."

"I will." I end the call and stay lying there for a moment, aware that I need to go and see Sam. I could tell he wasn't completely happy that it was Paul I was talking to.

I tread carefully up the stairs. Go into the bedroom, where Sam is pulling off his socks.

"Just putting some shorts on," he says. "Lovely day out there."

"It is," I agree.

"How was Paul?"

"He was fine. I was just filling him in on all the shit that's going on."

"Well, he seems to have cheered you up a bit."

"He…?" I feel like I need to tread carefully here.

"You were laughing away in there."

"Oh, he was just being an idiot. He said Shona might be able to help, actually." I am hoping that reminding Sam of

Paul's girlfriend – and showing him that Paul is trying to get me to work with her – will neutralise things.

"Oh, right."

"Don't be annoyed."

"I'm not annoyed."

I can tell he is. And what's more, I know exactly why. I have not been good company lately; preoccupied with everything, I don't suppose I have smiled or laughed all that much. So returning to find me laughing away down the phone with my ex – although really, Paul is barely that – has made him feel bad.

What Sam doesn't realise – because I haven't told him; I haven't told anyone, in fact – is that I am scared. My imagination is working overtime at the moment. What I keep thinking is that this person must have been here, to have taken those photos. Perhaps they really have stayed here before or, much worse, maybe they have been here specifically to take the pictures. I try to push this thought from my mind and I don't want to voice it to anybody else. It feels like it would make that possibility more real.

Amethi no longer feels the safe place it once did.

I go up to Sam, slip my arms around him. "I'm sorry," I say. "This is meant to be our best time yet. And if I haven't told you before how happy I am that you're here, then I'm an idiot. I feel like I've been waiting for this my whole life."

I look into his eyes and see them connect properly with me, his expression softening. He kisses me and pulls me close. "I just want to make you happy," he says.

"You do. You must know that. You really do."

15

"I feel like you're becoming obsessed by this, Alice," David says, trying and failing to open a childproof bottle of medicine. Tyler has got a cold and is feeling miserable, his round little cheeks more apple-like than ever, shiny and red as they are. Lying against David, his eyes are on me and I wonder what he makes of this conversation. Probably that it is interminably dull.

"Here," Martin takes the bottle from David and rolls his eyes at me. "There's a reason you can't open childproof things, David."

"Yes, because I've managed to keep my youthfulness."

"Oh yes, of course, that must be it." Martin draws some of the sweet, sticky liquid into a plastic syringe and Tyler's mouth opens like a baby bird's. In goes the medicine and Tyler sinks back against David.

"There you go, young man. Soon be feeling better. This stuff is like magic." Martin screws the lid back on the bottle.

"You do it too tight!" David says. "No wonder I can't open it."

"I thought it was because you had the secret elixir of youth?"

"Alright, baldie, no need for jealousy."

"Baldie!" Tyler giggles; the first time I've seen him laugh since I've been here.

It's a Sunday and Sam is working; he and Sophie have

gone off to Falmouth, where there's a regatta today. They are doing some awareness work with the public and Sophie's excited because the *Cornish Tribune* might be there. When David invited me to lunch, I jumped at the chance.

"I'm not obsessed," I say now, unwilling to let the subject drop. Tyler wriggles against David, as if trying to get even closer, if that were possible.

"Alice, lovely, I can see it's driving you mad. And I get it, I really do. But remember what they say about bullies. Turn the other cheek. But more importantly than that, just try to put it in perspective. This is one person – right? Posting things on social media, most of which get taken down. You've seen a few cancellations but are there more than there would normally be?"

"A few more," I say sullenly, not wanting this played down.

"But you're doing OK, still – you and Julie?"

"I guess."

Tyler pulls David's hand into his mouth.

"Urgh, don't suck my thumb! You've got two perfectly good ones of your own," David says but his grin is a mile wide. I can't help but smile to see him so happy. Tyler giggles. "What I'm trying to say, Alice," David moves smoothly back to the original topic, cleaning his thumb with a baby wipe, "is yes, it's horrible. But it's not affecting anything too badly. The business is strong. And look at the way all your other customers are jumping to your defence. But Tyler," David looks like he's just remembered something, "you need to stop sucking anyone's thumbs, even your own, or your teeth will grow crooked."

This is true; both about the teeth and about the loyalty so many people have shown towards Amethi. After Angie George have come lots of other people who have stayed with us, who have seen the nastiness and responded, with glowing testimonials, refuting the claims which this mystery reviewer – CornwallLover1242… Jeff Halford… whoever – has made.

Julie seems to be letting all this roll off her back, but then it's not targeting her so closely. Sam is annoyed by it all but thinks it's best to get on with it. I could not possibly tell Mum and Dad how I feel because they'll just worry about me. I remember Dad wasn't keen on me living up at Amethi on my own, back when Julie and I first got the place. He'll want me to move in with them or something. At least it is different now that Sam is with me.

Nevertheless, the nastiness, the cheap insults, and particularly the photos, are affecting how I feel about my own home.

"I know," I sigh. "And you're right, I am becoming a bit obsessed. Let's change the subject, shall we? Tyler doesn't want to listen to all this, do you?"

The little boy has dozed off, his mouth puckered open sweetly, allowing a small amount of drool to drizzle onto David's jeans.

"Urgh," David says quietly, grabbing a baby wipe – there are packets of these in every room in the house these days, it seems – and wiping his leg gently. But his eyes are on Tyler and he's smiling.

Martin comes back into the room. His eyes, too, fall on their son, and his expression softens. "Lunch is ready," he whispers. "Maybe we'd better leave Ty here."

David manages to extricate himself from the little boy, easing a cushion into the place where he had been and pulling a small soft blanket over the sleeping child. We quietly go through to their conservatory, which has a view over the estuary. The tide is out, the shallows glistening in the sunshine, dotted with wading birds and black headed gulls just chilling out in the heat of the day.

"I love this room," I say. "I do miss being right by the sea."

"But Amethi is so beautiful," Martin places two strips of baked aubergine on my plate then passes me a bowl of salad. "I'd love somewhere like that, with a bit more land."

The garden here is sculpted, on three levels to incorporate the slope of the plot.

"I used to love my little courtyard," says David, tearing a piece of bread and putting some into his mouth. "A proper sun trap, that was enough garden for me. I love Amethi too but the thought of having to maintain all that space… no thanks."

"It's not too bad," I laugh. "Why do you think we've put in the wildflower meadows? Anyway, Dad likes to come and give us a hand with all that. I think he misses the garden he and Mum had back home."

"Hey, it's not home – it's where you used to live. This is home," David taps the table.

"Sorry – where we used to live," I correct myself. "And of course, he loves the little courtyard at your old house. I think he falls asleep there almost every afternoon."

"Sleep," Martin says dreamily. "I remember that."

"And sleeping during the day!" exclaims David. "Did we used to do that?"

"If we felt like it," Martin says. "But we never needed to. Because we'd normally slept in till mid-morning. God, those days seem like a different lifetime."

"Weekends away… uninterrupted dinners…" David recalls.

"Uninterrupted nights' sleep."

"Disposable income."

"No disposable nappies."

"You wouldn't have it any other way," I exclaim. "I can see how happy you are as parents. And you're so good at it."

"I don't know about that," Martin says modestly.

"The way you got that medicine into Tyler, as if it was second nature. And the way he was snuggling up to you, David. It feels like he's always been yours."

"Thank you, Alice," I can see David's eyes shining. "Sorry. I feel like I've been so much more emotional since I've been a parent."

"And fearful," Martin says ruefully. "I can hardly bear to watch the news and see the world our little boy is growing up in."

"Well, you're great – both of you. And Tyler obviously feels very secure and settled." I raise my glass of sparkling apple juice. "To both of you, and Tyler."

Martin and David raise their glasses to join mine, pride and joy shining on both their faces. I am glad I've come to see them. Taking a break has helped me put things in perspective, as Sam said it would; it's given me a little bit of breathing space. Sometimes there is nothing like the company of good friends to put things right with the world. I drop in to see Mum and Dad on the way back, parking near the top of the road and tracing the familiar path down to the house where I first lived when I came to Cornwall. I remember turning up with Julie that very first time, heavy bags gratefully dropped on the pavement; her brashly ringing the doorbell; both of us waiting, unsure what to expect when the door was opened. Our relief and joy when David's face was revealed, smiling and welcoming.

That golden summer, which lasted three months but felt like forever. Then ten years later we were back again, in the same tiny rooms at the top of the house, until David moved in with Martin, and Julie and I were promoted to the larger rooms on the middle floor. I have got used to Mum and Dad living here now, and I love being able to revisit my little room at the top of the house. Open the tiny window and feel the breath of the sea on me; hear the gulls shrieking and the happy voices of holiday makers traipsing down the hill on their way to the town.

I go up there now, while Mum's waiting for the kettle to boil. Dad is out somewhere; he's heard about a new organic farm shop somewhere along the coast.

"He's set himself another mission," Mum laughed. Dad regularly finds himself little tasks to perform, especially when Mum is working. Visiting the tin mines; researching and finding the best local dairies – even though I've told him Michael's is the place to go; booking himself on to tours of local vineyards. Many of his undertakings involve food in some way, although he claims it's the local angle he's interested in, not the delicious produce.

Mum is using this room as her craft room these days. The bed has gone; replaced by a heavy old desk. I know it's heavy because I helped move it up here. In the little nook under the window is an armchair (which I also helped to move) that Mum has upcycled beautifully. I sit for a minute, close my eyes. Breathe in.

I am so grateful to be able to come back here. No matter how much I love Amethi, there is something about this house and this room in particular which feels like home. I think it will always feel like home. *I can recentre here*, I think, knowing it sounds cheesy but I am not really sure how else to put it.

With the little window open, I lie my head back against the curve of the chair, breathe deeply. *In… out… in… out*, hearing Kate's voice in my head. *If your thoughts start to wander,*

134

bring them back to your breathing. To some people, a load of hippy claptrap. To me, absolute sense. I concentrate on my breathing, and I notice the slight whisper of the breeze across the top of my head; the voices and footsteps of people passing by on the street below; a sparrow chirping somewhere nearby, perhaps from the gutter of a neighbouring house. I feel centred. I feel calm. I...

"SQUARK! Squ-squ-squ-squ-SQUARK!"

I am disturbed from my reverie by a gull who has perched literally on the open window and is shouting to all its mates. At my movement, it rises rapidly; large wings spreading into the sky. Ah well, I shouldn't leave Mum too long anyway. She'll be wondering what I'm up to.

I find her sitting in the garden, browsing through the local paper. "I thought you'd fallen asleep up there," she smiles. On the table in front of her is a tray with a pot of tea; proper teacups and saucers; a plate of Fox's Classic biscuits.

"My favourites!"

"I know," she smiles. "It's nice to see you looking relaxed. You need to make the most of your Sundays, you know."

"I do," I reassure her as I sit down, aware of the scent of flowers on the warm air and the sun on my skin. "Sometimes I just feel like being at home, though."

"I can imagine – the only thing is, for you home is also work. I bet you get guests coming and asking for things if you're at home."

"Sometimes, but I don't mind."

"I know you don't but you still need to take a step away from it every now and then. Did you have a nice lunch?"

"Lovely. But Tyler isn't well." I describe how he was snuggled into David, and how efficient Martin was at dealing with the medicine. "How do you know what to do?" I muse. "If you're a parent, and your child is ill, how

135

do you know how ill they are, and when you should call a doctor, and how much medicine to give them?"

"It's like everything else about being a parent," Mum laughs. "You do your best, and you learn as you go along. And if you're lucky, you have people around who can help. Martin's mum and dad are supportive, aren't they?"

"I think so. I'm sure of it, in fact. David says it's a myth, the whole interfering in-laws thing."

"Ha! Well that probably depends on the in-laws." Mum smiles. "I was lucky, with Grandma Griffiths."

"If anything, he says it's Bea who's a pain. And she hasn't even had kids herself!"

"I can just imagine what Bea's like. She loves that little boy, doesn't she? And I can see how proud she is of David – I was watching her up at the Cross Section the other week."

"She's like a proud mum, isn't she?"

"I'd say she's probably a typical older sister. And she hasn't got kids of her own so Tyler's the closest thing."

"But how did you know, Mum?" I persist.

"Know what?

"What to do? How to be a mum?"

"Honestly, I just made it up – or asked for advice – or read books. And tried to do the right thing. And probably worried I'd done the wrong thing, a lot. Why? You're not…?"

"No! Nothing like that." I want to tell her that Julie and Luke are trying for a baby but it's not my secret to tell.

"Good. I mean, not good – if that's what you want, then you should go for it. But Sam's only just back, and it seems like a good thing for you and he to have some time together, just the two of you. You've certainly earned it."

I change the subject now. Mum always draws things out of

me and I almost always think afterwards that I have not asked her about herself; her life. She and Dad have done a big thing, moving from the town they have lived in all their lives – and I almost forget that Mum was ill a couple of years ago. So ill that both Dad and I thought we were going to lose her.

"How are you, Mum?" I ask now.

"Oh, I'm fine!" she laughs. "You know me."

The way her eyes leave mine, just momentarily, does not escape my attention.

"Mum?" I ask suspiciously.

"Well, it's just… work. I don't think I like it very much, to be honest."

"Oh no, Mum. You've never said anything about it before." Probably because I've just talked about myself all the time, I think.

"It's nothing major; hardly worth mentioning, really. But I suppose I don't really feel like I fit in. It's just a small office, you know, and the others have all worked there for a long time. You can tell they know each other inside out, and I don't suppose I have that much in common with them, either."

"That sounds a bit miserable."

"It's not miserable, exactly. They're perfectly pleasant. But I feel like an outsider, I suppose."

Mum's is a new job at the hospice and I think a couple of her colleagues had applied for it so I don't suppose that helps her position.

"But it's nothing to worry about, Alice. And there are lots of things I love about it; spending time with the families is inspirational. And humbling. And I don't have to work. You know I just don't want to retire! But it means I don't feel completely tied to the job. Not like some people who have to work to survive. I'm lucky."

"Does Dad know you don't like it?"

"Yes, he told me to tell my colleagues to go and stuff themselves."

We both laugh.

"Really, they're not awful. I suppose I was used to working at the same place for so long. Maybe I was just as bad when somebody new started at the old place."

"I doubt it, somehow."

We sink into a comfortable silence. Mum wriggles her shoes off, closes her eyes and turns her face to the sun. I pull another garden chair across and sit back down, resting my feet on the second chair. David is right about this little garden being a sun trap. And like the rest of this house, it holds many memories for me. I sit for a while and let them wash over me.

By the time I get home, I feel thoroughly recharged and ready to face anything. I send David and Martin a quick text to thank them for lunch and enquire after Tyler. **Already back on his feet and terrorising us**, Martin is quick to reply.

Ha ha, excellent.

David is having a kip. He's working tomorrow and he was up all with night with Ty.

You two have it all sorted! Give D my love when he wakes. Make sure you get some rest too.

I don't need rest, didn't you know I'm super-human?

I had heard a rumour… xx

See you soon Alice. And DO NOT let the internet weirdo get to you. It will all blow over soon. You and Julie have an amazing place and loads of happy customers. Who knows what motivates people? You just be proud of what you're doing and carry on being your friendly, cheerful, helpful self. That way you win and 'Jeff' is just some sad little person with nothing better to do than send spiteful messages xxx

Martin's message makes me smile but it does also bring my mind back to focus on the problem. I had promised myself I wouldn't check social media today but I can't help myself. Even as I'm opening the laptop I am telling myself it's not too late to stop, but I carry on.

I see immediately that there is another review on TripRecommends.co.uk and as the cartwheel rating has reduced to 4.0 I am guessing it is not a good one.

1 out of 5 cartwheels
Anonymous
I would give 1.5 stars if I could because the food is good. **My recent stay at Amethi was nothing short of abysmal. I arrived to find the place I had booked had not been cleaned since the last people had left and the owner or manager or whatever she is was sitting having a cigarette. I complained immediately and received a very rude answer. The location is nice and the food too but the management are too young to run a place like this. Some people don't deserve their lives.**

Wow. That last sentence hits me right in the gut. What the hell does that mean, and what is this if not intensely personal? Who is doing this, and why? It feels like the more positive reviews we get, the worse these bad ones become.

It's not the first time that our age has been mentioned and I realise that thirty-two might seem young to some people but it's not like we're teenagers. And between us, Julie and I have a good few years' experience. But then it's not really Julie who's being got at.

I am at once annoyed at myself for looking, allowing my day to be ruined, and at the same time shocked and upset. I realise I am shaking. Checking the clock, I can see it's going to be another couple of hours before Sam gets back.

Ping.

An email arrives in the inbox. It is from Colin Haygarth; one of the writers who was with us a few weeks back, who left that lovely review.

Dear Alice and Julie,
I don't know if you will remember me from the writing course in June but I had a blast and I've kept in touch with some of the writers – and the tutors. I was very sorry to hear from Rosie about the nasty comments some idiot is posting on the internet.

There is clearly no truth in them and I've been in touch with a couple of the people, and we are going to respond to all such comments, truthfully. Helen and Tony in particular are keen to get involved, and I have been talking to Tony about coming down to stay with you guys again;

perhaps in the autumn, if you have availability? We're both young (well he is), free and single, and want to get on with our writing. I have plans to finish my novel while I know he wants to get back to some of the short stories he started while he was there. We can't think of anywhere we'd rather be to write than at Amethi.

If you have any two-bed accommodation free, please let me know.

Best wishes,

Colin Haygarth

Colin's email does something to neutralise the poison I feel is flooding through my veins, and very shortly afterwards I notice that he has responded to the recent TripRecommends review, and very forcefully. It is lovely of him but I feel embarrassed that he feels he needs to jump to our assistance.

I shut the laptop down; I should never have opened it anyway, and I lie back on the sofa, trying to calm myself with the breathing exercises but I am too agitated.

No – fuck it, I suddenly find myself thinking. I am not taking this. I have done nothing wrong, and I deserve none of this. Neither does Julie. I am going to go out and have a wander about this beautiful place where I live and work. If I bump into some of the guests I am going to smile and chat, as I always would. Whoever this is – assuming it is just one person – is not going to get me down any longer. They are not going to win.

16

"You don't think it could be this Colin geezer, do you?"

I look at Sam. The thought had not even crossed my mind. But shit... what if it is? The timing...

"He's an older bloke," I say, scanning my memory for any clues Colin may have given when he was here. I can't think of anything. "Maybe he's just a slightly deranged man, who has a problem with young women."

"Young successful women," Sam says.

It doesn't fit with my memory of Colin, somehow. He really did seem to be the 'what you see is what you get' type. But of course, I met him fleetingly over a few days. Not enough time to get to know him properly. But also surely not enough time for him to have developed this problem with me? I feel like somebody should get to know me properly before they decide they hate me. It's the least I deserve.

"I'm not sure, Sam. I really can't picture Colin doing this."

"But you don't know. That's the problem with this place. You have strangers coming week in, week out. You don't know who they are and you're open and friendly and accommodating. I used to worry about you when I was up in Bangor. All alone here with a bunch of strangers."

"Did you?" I smile, kind of liking the idea of Sam worrying about me.

"Yes."

"But what's the difference between living with strangers up here and living with strangers in a street, or a block of flats? You don't normally know your neighbours when you move into a new place."

I know this argument because it's one I've had internally a number of times. Sam correctly chooses the next point.

"But when you move home, it's into a place you've been able to check out, if you're lucky. And you should be there long enough to get to know those people you live near. Here, and I am not saying this to worry you, you've got new people every week. And it's secluded, too. Now I do sound like I'm trying to scare you. I promise I'm not. And anyway, I'm here now."

"My big man, come to protect me," I grin.

"Don't," Sam says, his brow lowering. "I'm not like that."

"I know you're not," I say, laying my head on his shoulder. "And I know you're right. But it's fine, and I've never been scared here."

Until recently, I think but don't say. I am touched by Sam's protectiveness and I'd had no idea he felt that way while he was up in Wales. But the truth is, the people who have been to stay here are usually families, or groups of friends, and they're not interested in me. I am at best a friendly figure to ask for help and give them a hand organising days out, restaurant bookings, taxis, etc. Otherwise, they are too busy enjoying themselves, squeezing as much relaxation and fun out of their time away, to really notice me.

I wonder if Sam has had the same thoughts I have about the pictures which were posted online - who took them, and when? An involuntary shudder passes through me.

"I'm sorry, Alice, I don't mean to make you feel worse."

"Don't worry, you haven't."

"But have you thought about calling the police?"

"And saying what? Somebody is saying mean things about me?"

"You're right, I'm sorry. I think maybe I'm becoming neurotic now!"

"Hey, are you saying I've been neurotic?"

"What? No! Of course not." He is laughing now.

"I tell you what, I'll reply to Colin and see what he has to say. I almost don't want him to come now."

"Sorry, Alice, it's probably nothing to do with the poor bloke! Go on, email him back, and book him and his mate in."

Dear Colin,

Thank you so much for your email and your kindness. It's really good to hear that you have kept in touch with the course tutors and some of the other writers. I rarely find out what happens after the courses here so it's lovely to think that people are making friendships which last.

Don't worry about the online comments. I don't.

We have availability in September in one of the two-bed places – a choice of two weeks:

7th – 13th or 20th – 27th.

If you want to speak to Tony and decide which is better, that would be great.

We look forward to hearing from you soon.

With best wishes for now,

Alice and Julie

I often sign off from the both of us – although Julie said it makes us sound like a couple.

"Well, we pretty much are," I said.

"You wish!"

Sam reads the email and gives his approval before I send it. He particularly likes the line about not worrying about the online stuff. "If it is him, that should annoy him!"

"I don't think we should pin it on Colin; or start thinking that it's him, otherwise we might develop an intense dislike of a perfectly nice man, and it will show when he's here. And if it's not him, he's being incredibly loyal to us and has only been here once."

"You're right. I'm sorry. I just want to know who the fuck is doing this stuff so we can put an end to it."

"But even if we find out, how are we going to stop it? I don't really think it's a police matter."

Unless somebody has been snooping.

"You're right."

"Anyway, I've decided to hell with it. I'm not letting this ruin anything anymore. I've had enough of it eating away at me and making me a misery. And one of the things I want to do is get Sophie up here and get decorating that room! I said we'd do it, and it's been weeks now. I'd like to get it all sorted before Kate's baby arrives – so Sophie has a refuge if the baby cries all night."

"She would love that." Sam kisses me.

"I'll text her in a minute."

"Text?" Sam says. "Alright, Grandma. I usually communicate with her on What'sApp."

"Ooh… *I usually communicate with her on What'sApp,*" I mimic. "You really think that's what the kids are doing these days? Face it, Sam, we're both getting old and outdated."

"Speak for yourself."

Sophie seems really excited at the thought of doing her room. This is also a good kick up the bum for me to finally go through all the stuff that's accumulated over the years, which Mum and Dad had kept for me and which they insisted I now take responsibility for so they didn't have to move it into their new house.

When Sophie stays with us, she has to share the room with boxes of folders and books from school and university; stuffed toys and trinkets gathered over the years; old clothes and photographs; stacks of reading books which I haven't been able to fit onto the shelves.

I can't believe I've managed to force my own hand into sorting this out but we can't redecorate until it's done.

I look into the room now; there are boxes stacked on top of the wardrobe, out of sight under the bed, and boldly standing out in the open, against the wall. I sigh. But it's about time this happened.

"I know what you're like," says Sam. "You are absolutely not allowed to go 'oh, but I still want this' about everything and end up with two books to give to a charity shop."

"Fine," I pretend-huff. "How about you help me, then?"

"Dammit. I asked for that, didn't I?"

"Yes, you did," I turn and give him what I think is a winning smile.

"Go on, then. No time like the present. I'll make us some coffee and we can get a couple of hours done before bed."

"Really?" I hadn't actually meant to begin right now.

"Yes, really! Little and often, or it will never happen."

"Alright, Grandma," I echo his earlier words.

He trots happily downstairs and I walk into the room, sit on the bed and look around me. What have I let myself in for?

17

This is my worst kind of activity. I take in the sight of the boxes and I don't know where to start, but start I must.

I brush a spindly, paper-thin dead spider off the nearest box, trying to extricate myself from its sticky, dusty web, which has stuck to the cardboard. I open the top of the box. Folders. This is my university work. I look at it, slightly guiltily, thinking how much time and effort I put into all this, and for what? Well, a degree, I suppose, but I must have forgotten more than half of what I learned at uni. Which brings into question just how useful a degree is. But I don't have time for that now.

I flick through pages of neatly typed essay, and test exam papers. Am I ever going to need these again? It seems unlikely. But it's hard to let go of years of work and these tie me to a very intense time in my life – of having lost Sam, and gained Geoff; though how much of a gain that was is questionable – when I was deeply unhappy and yet finding my feet as an independent almost-adult. As ever, when I think of Geoff, I feel uncomfortable, partly at the way I let him treat me but more at the way that he ended his life. He was only in his mid-twenties. No age at all. And I didn't hate him, but he was not good for me and I am sure he would only have carried his controlling ways with him into a new relationship.

It was only years later that I discovered he'd sent Sam – who had tracked me down – packing, and I never had any idea that he had come looking for me.

But Geoff could have sorted these aspects of his personality out, I'm sure of it. If he'd wanted to, he could have seen a counsellor, got to the root of whatever his problem was. I wonder if I could have, or should have, helped him. While I know he wasn't my responsibility, it is hard to feel that or truly believe it. He needed help and perhaps I should have been the one to provide it.

I flick through each folder, transported back nearly fifteen years, to my student room; walls messily covered in photos of my school days, and uni friends, and nights out, and more than a few of beautiful Cornwall. I did not put any pictures of Sam on my wall but I had them tucked neatly away in a book. I wonder where all those pictures are now. Very possibly in one of these boxes.

I need to be ruthless. I take out each polythene pocket and extract the pages and pages of paper, piling them into the box, destined for the recycling. I will have to work out a plan for the ring binders later.

Box two. I smile when I open this. It's like a little shrine to my childhood. A musical jewellery box, which I was so excited to get for my eighth birthday. I lift the lid and a tiny ballerina pops up. With a little twist of the handle at the back, she begins to dance, to the tune of *Raindrops Keep Falling on My Head*. Even the old pieces of jewellery are in here. Some are plastic; remnants of long-forgotten birthday parties, but there are also some bracelets which my Grandma Gladys – Mum's mum – gave me. I lift them out, letting the cheap beads run through my fingers like I used to do, remembering how I loved the phrase 'dripping with jewels' and used in more than once in creative writing at school, until kind Miss Treece suggested I might branch out a bit.

"Just as I suspected." Sam's voice jolts me from my reverie. "Here," he hands me a coffee. "You're never going to get any of this done if you take an hour looking at everything you find. Put the jewels back in the box. No arguments," he interrupts, seeing me about to protest.

I do as I'm told.

"Now, you need to get some boxes for things that you want to keep. And boxes for things to get rid of."

"I've started using that for recycling," I indicate the box that held my uni work.

"Excellent. Now, I know exactly what you're like, and I'm going to help. We'll do another hour tonight, shall we?"

"OK, boss," I smile, thinking it might be quite useful to have him telling me what to do in this instance.

"You go through your box of junk."

"Hey, I'll have you know these are treasures from my childhood."

"Sure. And they're going to come in useful, are they?"

"They might, if we…" The words are nearly out of my mouth but I bite them back.

Sam just smiles. "Well, see what you really want to keep. I reckon there's a little more space in the loft if we do some careful reorganising – but only things that you *really want*."

"Ok, ok."

We work quietly for a while. Sam occasionally holds something up for me to say yes or no to, but makes it his business to weed out anything which is extraneous. He also happens across a box of pans.

"Those are the ones Mum was looking for when they moved in!" I say. "She's bought all new ones now."

"So could these be of use to Julie?"

"Possibly…"

"Or shall I stick them in the charity shop pile?"

"Let's check with Julie first."

I am busy working out which primary school books I want to keep. "I can't believe you've got your primary school books!" Sam had exclaimed. "I've got next to nothing from that time in my life." I'm tempted to say that's more down to his mum not keeping things than him being better organised than me, but I know that's not fair. He has an OK relationship with his mum, who lives in Spain, but from what he's said it doesn't seem like she was all that supportive of him growing up. He had a lot of freedom but it perhaps wasn't what he wanted, or needed.

I sense a shift in Sam suddenly and I look up. I see immediately what he's looking at.

"Have I still got that?" I rush to say. He's holding a little menu and a note, from Paul. Damn, I think. They are from the night that we went out to that posh country club hotel on the other side of the county. It was a lovely night. Paul had put the menu and note in my bag without my realising; in fact, I hadn't found them till weeks later, having let the old tissues and half-finished packs of chewing gum accumulate for long enough. I had fished out the menu and found the note:

A little memento of a beautiful evening. I hope we can repeat it again soon.
P xxx

We never did repeat it, and by the time I'd found the note I'd already decided that there was no future for Paul and me. I curse myself now for not just getting rid of them both.

"Yes," Sam says drily. "You have."

"Well look, it's from ages ago – one of the handful of

dates I went on with Paul. Look, the receipt's stapled to the menu, you can see the date on it."

"Not short of a few bob, is he?" Sam says, eyeing the receipt. I know this had bothered him before; particularly when he'd wanted to take me up to see Mum in hospital and his car was in the garage but Paul had turned up in his flash, shiny convertible, ready to go.

"Well, no," I say now, "but we already knew that. And yes, it was a lovely place and the food was excellent, but you know that doesn't matter."

"Sorry," Sam says.

"Don't be. I should have binned that."

"Recycled it," Sam smiles.

"That's what I meant. Anyway, somewhere in the midst of all this stuff is a box rammed full of things from that first summer I spent down here. I kept everything to do with you. Receipts, lolly wrappers, corks and beer bottle tops. I'll dig it out and bore you with it all."

"It's a nice offer, but I'll pass." Sam grins. "Did you really keep all that stuff?"

"Yes," I say, "I did."

"Weirdo."

"I can't win, can I?"

With Sam's excellent management skills, we get through about a third of the boxes.

"Don't look!" he says, at the pile that has accumulated behind him. "If these were things you needed, you'd have realised by now."

"This is tough, I can't believe I'm letting you make these executive decisions on my behalf."

"I'll let you throw out my old socks if you like."

"No, it's fine. I will not be one of those women who

151

governs what their partner wears, even if it means having to put up with the socks you've had since you were sixteen."

"They're not that bad! Now come on, let's leave all this stuff, and let's get to bed."

"OK, if you insist."

Sam leaves the room first and as I switch the light off I cast my eye over the piles of my old belongings. Sam is right; keep the things which mean something and bin all the rest. It's ridiculous to keep so much, I know, but it is also hard to let go.

18

While I am showering the next morning, Sam is loading his car with the things we'd earmarked for the charity shop. "Before you change your mind," he grins at me when I arrive downstairs to see him carrying the last box out.

"You're a cruel man," I say.

"Harsh but fair, I like to think. And Sophie is really excited that we're doing this."

"Oh OK, then. I wouldn't want to let her down."

"I know. And I thought you and she might like to go on a shopping trip next Sunday, to get the stuff. I've got a few things I want to do with Luke, if you don't mind."

"What are you two up to?" Luke and Sam are almost like brothers and it seems ridiculously cosy that my best friend is married to Sam's. That all happened so quickly; while Sam and I have been going through all of our trials and tribulations, Julie and Luke managed to form a relationship and get married, with almost no troubles at all, apart from a slight blip caused by Julie's ex-fiancé, oh and the time that she proposed to Luke and he said no. Now they're trying for a baby. It never ceases to amaze me, how life turns out sometimes.

When Sam has gone to work I wander over to the office, waving to Mr Washington, who is lugging a cool-box in the direction of the car park, a further two bags slung over his shoulders.

"Day out?" I ask cheerfully.

"Yes, we thought we'd try that beach you recommended. But I was hoping to catch you, Alice; we were wondering about the Eden Project. Is it worth a visit?"

"Definitely. Maybe a good day this week would be Wednesday as it looks like it might be a bit overcast. Do you want me to sort out some tickets for you?"

"Would you?"

"Of course. And do you need anything else sorting?"

"No, that's fine. I don't want to put you to any bother."

It's a funny thing – one of our 'unique selling points', as annoying people like to call them, is that we will take the hassle out of a holiday. On top of Julie cooking five nights out of the seven each week, we can provide things like ticket booking, arranging taxis, nights out, tables at restaurants; often with a discount, thanks to the local business network. Yet often people seem to feel awkward asking us for anything.

I had worried when we set the business up that people would ask too much; I might get annoyed at the type of person who wanted such luxury arrangements, and demanded such a level of service, but by and large this has not been my experience at all.

"Well, if you think of anything, just let me know," I say now. "In fact, do you want me to carry one of those for you?"

"Oh no, of course not. You must have lots to do. But thanks for the offer."

"No problem," I smile and continue on my way. I feel lighter now, somehow, than I have for weeks. My resolve to stand firm in the face of the recent negativity is holding. It is tested, however, when I switch my computer on and see that I have two cancellations to deal with, one of them stating they have changed their minds having seen some of the recent online reviews. At least they're being honest.

I reply to the two emails, politely, wondering how to word my response to the one that mentions the TripRecommends website. I type out a few lines, delete them, try again. Repeat. Eventually I go with:

I am very sorry that you have taken this decision based on the few negative reviews online. However, I fully understand that when you are booking a holiday you need to be sure that your time away is the best it can be. I realise how precious holidays are and we do our utmost at Amethi to ensure our guests have a wonderful break. The majority of reviews are testament to this. I hope that you will consider us again in the future.

Don't rise to it, I tell myself. *Remember your promise the other night.* I sit up straight in my chair, hold my chin up, remind myself of the breathing exercises. Go to the web browser. Type in 'TripRec…' and the search engine fills in the rest for me. I click on it. I'm an idiot. I can't help myself.

Overall rating: 3.7 cartwheels. Shit. We haven't gone below four before. And I am well aware how ridiculous it seems to be judging our own success on a number of virtual cartwheels. But unfortunately, this is how it works.

I see we have five new reviews, each one star. This is what has tipped the balance. I read each one, becoming increasingly agitated. I feel like my stomach is in knots. Any idea of deep breathing goes out of the window.

One out of five cartwheels
Anonymous
DO NOT STAY
I don't know where to start with this 'luxury self-catering complex' so all I can say is – don't do it!!!!

One out of five cartwheels
Anonymous
Terrible Service
Nice place and gr8 food but manager is rude.

One out of five cartwheels
Anonymous
Age before beauty
I mention that saying because if you stay at Amethi you will notice it is a beautiful place to be, in a wonderful location, but also that the management are very young and arguably too young to have taken on such a venture.

While an excellent idea, one can't help feeling that Alice Griffiths has bitten off more than she can chew.

I feel sick to my stomach. The way it is written suggests that this person knows me although, conceivably, it might just be a clever use of my name which is of course on the website, alongside Julie's. This, I might be able to get TripRecommends to remove, arguing it breaches some kind of privacy. I pick up the phone and ring Julie, reading the next review while I listen the ring tone at the other end of the line.

One out of five cartwheels
Anonymous
Disappointing
We paid above the odds for a luxury holiday, having had a hard year as a family with the death of one of my parents. I was looking forward to a week away in my favourite part of the country, and to having somebody else manage things like days out, as promised in the marketing literature of 'Amethi'.

Despite repeated requests for help, with finding places to eat and booking tickets for days out, nothing was done and we were left to arrange everything ourselves.

The accommodation was nice but nothing fancy and felt just like a holiday home.

I can imagine this convincing potential customers – and I'm surprised we've only had two cancellations.

Julie's phone goes to voicemail. I leave a message, knowing how glum my voice will sound, but unable to breathe any levity into it:

"Hi Julie, it's me. Sorry, I had to call somebody. I know you're think I'm obsessed with this but look at TripRecommends. Somebody has been really busy over the weekend."

One out of five cartwheels
Anonymous
Drity [sic]
I seen a post by someone on Facebook with pics of piles of rubbish and I got some of my own. This place is dirty and not luxury.

157

Attached to this review are two images, taken from just by the car park. They make my heart hammer and I'm annoyed at myself for allowing my resolve to crumble just like that. One is similar to that first photo on Facebook, with convincing details like the overflowing bins in the car park. I wish I'd taken screenshots of those previous pictures, before Julie got the group admin to remove them.

The other two are of discarded furniture amongst long, unkempt grass; a mattress, a chair, and a pair of what look like bedside lamps. It is clear to me that these photos have not been taken here, and might well be of somebody's fly-tipping in a layby somewhere.

I go to phone Sam but I stop myself. He will be at work. And I haven't done very well at getting over all this stuff if I fail and phone him, crying, at the first hurdle. Because I am crying now. I don't know if the tears are of sorrow, anger or frustration. I suspect a mix of all three.

How do I fight this stuff? And why is it directed at me?

These five reviews are quite different; enough so to appear to be written by different people. This could easily be achieved by somebody who can write, though. Colin comes to mind, briefly – then Shona. She works in PR, she'll be highly practised at copy-writing. I shrug both thoughts away. As all the reviews are anonymous, they should be less than convincing. And if a reader was so inclined, they could click on the reviewer profile and find that these were their only reviews. But the thing is, there are so many places to choose from, and people are so used to scrolling through websites, or narrowing their options down to best rated on a website, that this new average score of Amethi's might just put us out of the running.

I feel hot, and flustered. The room seems suddenly small and I open the window wider, let some air in. Try very,

very hard to practise those breathing techniques.

Clicking back to the photo of Amethi I scour it, looking for clues. The hanging baskets at the corner of the building are just visible and I can see the pink and purple petunias trailing from them. This means this is a recent photo.

Dad has only just hung those for us, less than two weeks ago. He hadn't been happy with the plants we had in them and so had taken them all back to his and Mum's; put in the petunias and nursed them until they were in full flower. Brought them up here with detailed instructions about the type of compost they like, and how often to water them.

Then my heart jumps into my mouth. I recognise one of the cars in the parking lot. It's Paul's.

19

I don't know what to do. Why is Paul's car on our car park? This photo is definitely from the last two weeks, and he hasn't been here recently – or I didn't think he had. I look more closely – try to work out the time of day, but I am not that much of a super sleuth. I want to phone him, but what am I going to say?

Luckily, I am rescued from these thoughts by Julie calling back.

"Alice, what's up?" she asks. "Sorry I missed you, I was just out running."

I miss running, I realise. I used to go regularly. I belonged to a club when I was back in the Midlands. It's a great way to reduce stress, and I could do with that now.

"Did you listen to my message?"

"No, sorry, I thought it would be quicker to call you straight back."

"OK. Are you anywhere near a computer?"

"Yes, Luke's. Why?" she asks suspiciously.

"The reviews, on the website." I find I am pulling myself back from further tears. "There are more of them."

"On TripRecommends?"

"Yes."

"OK, OK." From her tone, I can tell Julie knows I'm upset. She goes quiet and I can hear the clicking of the keyboard. "Hang on…" she goes quiet again. "OK."

I give her a moment to read them. "Shit," she says once,

160

then she says it again.

"Can you see the one with the pictures?" I ask, trying to pull myself together and sound business-like.

"Yep, just opening them."

"Fucking hell, I can't believe they're doing this again," Julie says.

"I know. Now take a look at the cars in the car park."

"Oh."

"Yes, oh."

"Is that…?"

"Yep."

"What the fuck?"

"I know. Now look at the hanging baskets."

"Oh yeah, they look good, don't they."

"I think you're missing the point, Julie. They've only looked like that for two weeks."

"Ohhh… I see what you mean."

"Yep. So somebody has been up here, taking photos. Now, it could be a guest who's been here recently…"

"Or it could be somebody who's made the trip up especially… But Paul?" she asks incredulously.

"Well, it looks like his car."

"Shame you can't see the registration."

"I know."

"Have you spoken to him lately?"

"No, not for a week or two." The last time was when Sam walked in at the tail end of our conversation.

"And would that have been before the hanging baskets went back up?"

"No, I think it was after that."

"This is weird. We definitely haven't had any guests with the same type of car?"

"I really don't think so. It's quite an unusual car, isn't it?"

161

"Yeah – well, Luke seems to think it's something special, anyway."

"How is Luke?" I find I just want to talk about something normal.

"Oh, fine. Well, actually, lying red-faced on the floor. I made him come for a run with me."

"Hey! You're not meant to be telling people things like that!" I hear Luke's indignant voice in the background.

"It's only Alice," Julie says, and the line goes muffled as I hear her saying something to him, presumably with her hand over the mouthpiece of the phone.

"Alice?" It's Luke now. "Are you OK?"

"I'm fine," I say. "Or just about."

"Well look, I know the guys who host TripRecommends, and they do all the content management, too. I don't know if Julie told you that. Do you want me to ask them to take these things down? Julie's up for it if you are."

"Could you?" I ask eagerly. Then, more doubtfully, "Should you?"

"You mean is it morally wrong? Should we let everybody have their say?" Luke laughs. "Look, Alice, if these seemed genuine then there's no way that I'd do that but they're obviously bollocks. And if they're affecting yours and Ju's business, they need to go."

"It just feels so…"

"Alice, this is not a level playing field. You are getting all this shit, with no way of fighting back. Let me have a word. Please."

"OK," I say. "As long as it's not massively unethical."

"It's not. Trust me. Would I do anything unethical?"

"No," I admit, "I don't suppose you would. Thank you, Luke."

And just like that, by the time evening has come around, all of the anonymous reviews have disappeared. This also means that a couple of positive ones have gone too, where people have forgotten – or deliberately omitted – to add their names but our rating is back to where it once was. 4.6 cartwheels. Just like that. I can't deny I'm relieved.

After dinner, Julie comes over. Sam lets her in.

"Hello," she kisses him on the cheek, "how's the new job?"

"Great," he grins widely. "I absolutely love it."

"I knew you would. And you bloody well deserve it, too. Is your beautiful girlfriend in?"

"I don't know where else I'd be!" I smile, coming into the hallway.

"Great. I just thought I'd let you know the reviews are all gone, in case you hadn't seen that."

"I did see, thank you Julie. And please thank Luke, as well."

"It's not a problem, at all. I did wonder if there was a conflict of interest with him being married to me but this isn't a fair war, or being played on a level playing field, or whatever. If they're fighting dirty then so should we."

"It sounds like Luke's managed to get them to put a filter on all the reviews for Amethi, too, so they can be reviewed manually before they're allowed on the site," Sam says.

"My brilliant husband," Julie says proudly.

"He is that," I agree. "But it does feel a bit uncomfortable. I guess it's not the same as paying for reviews."

"Exactly. It's not. And anything which isn't anonymous will get posted, negative or positive."

"I suppose that's not so bad." It still feels wrong.

"What about Paul's car, though?"

"What's this?" Sam asks. I hadn't told him this detail yet. Julie clearly realises her mistake but it's out there now.

"I was going to tell you," I say apologetically, "but we're not sure. It's just that one of the cars on that photo looks like Paul's."

"Really? You don't see many of them around."

"No," I try – and fail – to sound nonchalant.

"Have you asked him about it?"

"No, not yet." In truth, I hadn't wanted to mention it to Sam because we do seem to have had a bit of friction between us when it comes to Paul.

"Do you want me to?"

"No, I'll do it. Just trying to work out what to say."

"OK," Julie interjects, "well, after ruining your evening, I'll say my goodnights." She smiles apologetically at us.

"You haven't ruined anything," I say. "Thanks for coming over. I'll see you tomorrow."

I kiss Julie on the cheek and close the door. I look at Sam.

"Maybe you can tell me if you think it's Paul's car? I saved a screenshot."

"OK," he says.

It feels like a wall has come up between us and I am floundering to think of the best way to break it down again. There is nothing between me and Paul, I want to say – and I wonder if he is thinking that there is. I want to ask but I fear that in doing so I'm going to make things worse.

I open my laptop and retrieve the file. "Look," I say, "the hanging baskets. So it must have been recent."

"Oh yeah," Sam's attention is drawn to the image on the screen. "And yes, I'd say that's Paul's car."

"Damn."

"Does he often come up here?"

"No, Sam, he doesn't. And you should know that. I

164

haven't actually seen him in weeks. Maybe months."

Sam sighs. "I don't know what I'm meant to think."

"What you are *meant to think*, Sam, is that I am stuck in a nightmare. There seems to be somebody who has it in for me, for some unknown reason, and I don't know how to stop them doing what they're doing. Luke has been brilliant, but it is pure luck that he is in a position to do what he's done today. And I'm not all that comfortable with it anyway. On top of that, somebody has been taking photos of the place where I live and work, doctoring them and putting them online. The worst of it is, I don't know who is doing this, when they've been up here, and whether this is just the tip of the iceberg. If that is Paul's car," I feel myself deflate suddenly, "then rather than him making illicit visits to me as you seem to think, I'm worried that he is linked to what's going on."

Sam is watching me as I let out this torrent of words and I see his face transform; he has what I think of as his closed look to start off with – when he is annoyed but doesn't really want to admit it. He plays his cards close to his chest but becomes uncommunicative, and extremely frustrating. This rapidly changes, as he begins to understand what I am saying.

"Shit," he says into the sudden silence that follows my monologue. "Sorry."

"It's OK." I feel drained, and just want to go upstairs and curl up in our bed. Right now I don't care whether he joins me or not.

Sam puts his arms out, carefully pulling me to him. "Sorry," he says again, into my hair.

20

I plough on, regardless. After my little tirade, I did go up to bed, and Sam looked after me. I think he was feeling guilty. He brought me hot chocolate, and toasted crumpets with melted butter and honeycomb-honey. Then he sat on the edge of the bed.

"Bloody hell, Alice, I really am sorry, you know."

"It's fine. I get it. This is such a ridiculous situation, and it's getting even more so. I can't really believe it's happening, to be honest."

"I don't want to ask but are you going to call Paul?"

"I haven't decided yet. I mean, what am I meant to say?"

"You could tell him I saw him leaving the other week, but forgot to mention it. Give him a chance to say what he was doing here."

"I'll think about it. Right now, it feels like it's a damage limitation exercise. When I look at the planner for the next few months, it's like it hasn't changed since a few weeks ago. Most of the available weeks are still available. Some of the weeks which were booked aren't any more. Maybe there's truth in what whoever it is says. Perhaps I have taken on more than I can handle."

"That's bollocks," Sam said frankly. "It's making you doubt yourself, which, for whatever reason, seems to be the desired result."

"I think I just need to sleep, and hopefully see things more clearly in the morning."

"OK," Sam looked sad. "I hate seeing the way this is affecting you."

"Do you think I'm over-reacting?"

"No, I don't. This is pretty nasty. And I think it would knock anybody about. But just remember, you are not on your own with this. Julie is your business partner and you've got me and Luke looking out for you as well."

"I know. Thank you, Sam. I love you."

"I love you, too." He kissed my forehead, put his hand gently on the back of my neck and looked me in the eyes. "You and Julie and Amethi will be here for a good long time – way after this idiot gets bored and finds somebody new to torment. Now eat and drink, and get some sleep."

He walked softly downstairs and I did as I was told – ate the crumpets and drank the hot chocolate, although my mouth felt dry. But then, try as I might, I could not sleep. The same run of thoughts just kept playing, on repeat. Why was Paul's car in that picture? Was it really his? I felt like I was going mad as I lay awake long into the night, hours after Sam had come up and climbed softly into place next to me, thinking I would already be asleep. I didn't disabuse him of this notion and instead focused my thoughts on him for a bit of respite, feeling the bed move as he made himself comfortable then listening to his steady breathing slowing and deepening as sleep crept across him.

I tried to make myself sleep, taking an imaginary walk along the coastal path, conjuring up the heat of the sun beating down on me and the waves rolling in and out at the bottom of the cliffs. Tracking a familiar route in the hope it might relax me but my mind would not let go.

The thought occurred to me that all of this – going right back to Paul helping me and Julie get this place – could be an elaborate way to get back at me for rebuffing him.

Get real, I tell myself. *Paul is not like that.* Besides, how high is my opinion of myself to think that Paul could have been so upset at not being with me?

But lack of sleep, and stress, do strange things to the mind. I need to remember that, and keep a firm grasp on reality, until this is sorted out once and for all.

"I still think it's Shona," Julie says. "Think about it… she has access to Paul's car. She knew that he used to be into you, and if you'd stuck with him she wouldn't have had a snowball's chance in hell…"

"I really don't think so," I say, though I don't think I sound very convincing. The truth is, I don't know what I think any more. I don't pretend to be perfect but I am shocked that somebody seems to have a personal vendetta against me. I don't think I'm a nasty person and I generally try to be pleasant and respectful to people.

"I'm going to phone Paul," Julie says suddenly.

"No…" it's too late. The phone is in her hand and she's swung her office chair away from mine. I stare at the back of her chair, listening to her side of the conversation.

"Hi Paul."

"Good, thanks. How are you?"

"I know, it's been a while… no, no problems. Well, actually, there is something you might be able to help with. I'm just going to send you something on email."

The picture. She's sending him the picture!

"Have you got it? Great – if you open that attachment you'll see what I'm phoning about… that's it. Yeah, I know, it's been done pretty professionally. I'd be convinced, if I didn't know better… Alice is fine, thanks. A bit pissed off, of course… Yeah, I'll hand you over in a minute. But I just wanted to ask you something first. Is that your car, in the picture?"

There is a moment's silence.

"I thought so. Did you want to see me or Alice? Or could Shona have borrowed the car?"

I can hear Paul's voice now, and he sounds angry. Julie is quiet.

"I can understand all that, Paul, but you must see how this looks. That is a recent photo, it's being used to slag us off, and potentially ruin our business, and there's your car, right in shot."

More of the raised voice. Julie pulls the phone away from her ear a little and I can hear Paul's words.

"… can't believe you're accusing me, or Shona of this… What does Alice have to say? I want to speak to her."

Julie passes the phone to me, raising her eyebrows and shrugging. I take the phone, glaring at my friend.

"Hi, Paul. I'm sorry about that. I had no idea Julie was…"

"Yes, well, I'm pretty pissed off. I can't believe that you two think I might…"

"I don't… we don't," I am quick to try and defuse the situation. "It's just…"

"It's just that you're having a nightmare," Paul's voice softens slightly. "I can see that. But I would never. I could never. And neither would Shona," he asserts. "I know you hardly know her, but she's a lovely person. And she's also extremely confident, she doesn't see you as a threat, if that's what you're thinking."

My cheeks flush. I feel like an absolute idiot.

"But," he concedes, "it looks strange, that my car is up at Amethi; yep, definitely a bit odd. To confirm, yes, that is my car and it was both of us – Shona and me – who were up there."

"OK…"

"It was the other week, after we'd spoken. I knew you were going to be with David and Martin, and I brought Shona to see the place."

I don't say anything. I am not sure how I feel about this.

"I know you've said no whenever I asked you before but once I'd seen all that crap online, I was talking to Shona about it and she had a few ideas – to get you some positive publicity," he quickly adds.

"She…?"

"Yes, so I took her up to Amethi, when I knew you weren't going to be there. It was sneaky, I'm sorry, and I'm also sorry if it seems like I'm not respecting your wishes. But she's got loads of connections and I knew she'd love the place. I was right, and she would happily do some PR for you, at a greatly reduced rate – to start off with, at least. It would give you and Julie a real voice, against the cowardly bastard who's got it in for you. And even without all that going on, it could work wonders for Amethi. Shona was talking national media – glossy magazines, weekend supplements, maybe even TV. You should think about it."

I don't know what to say. So I just say, "I will."

"Can you tell Julie I'm sorry for losing my rag at her?"

"Yes, it's fine," I say. "In fact, why don't you tell her yourself?" I flick the speakerphone setting on.

"Julie, I'm sorry," says Paul. "You need to get Alice to fill you in on what I've just told you."

"Sure," says Julie, grinning at me.

"I don't like being accused of anything I didn't do," Paul says. "I don't mind if it's something I did do…"

"That's fair enough," says Julie. "And I'm sorry, too."

"It's OK. You two are having a tough time. It will make you stronger, as people and as a business – so try and remember that. I'll let you two talk and hopefully hear from one or both of you again soon."

"Bye, Paul."

Julie turns to me and I fill her in on what Paul has said.

"I can't believe you didn't tell me Shona offered to help before!" Julie exclaims. "Actually, I can totally believe it. But now she's knocked off the list of suspects, I can't see any reason not to say yes. Can you? I feel like we could do with all the help we can get right now."

"I agree," I say reluctantly. "I'll get Paul to put us in touch with her."

It feels, all of a sudden, like we are strengthening our team. Luke is looking out for us with the website. He's one line of defence. Now we might have Shona gunning for us. She's our attack. Meanwhile, Julie and I have to keep Amethi running, and keep positive.

I feel better, knowing that we are not powerless, but I am still determined to find out who has it in for me, and why.

21

"Is that Alice?"

"Speaking." I already know who it is, though it is not a number I'm familiar with. The soft Scottish lilt is a giveaway.

"It's Shona here, Alice. How are you?"

"I'm good, thanks. How are you?"

"Oh you know, busy as ever. Looking forward to a break in a few weeks' time."

"That sounds good, are you going anywhere nice?" Enough of the small talk, I'm thinking, but I can't be the one to move the conversation on.

"Paul and I are going to Thailand."

"That sounds great." Was the whole thing a set-up so that she could tell me she and Paul were going away? *Stop it*, I tell myself. *This woman is going to help you.* "

"Aye, it should be. But that's not why I called." *Isn't it?* "I was really thrilled to see your place the other week. It is absolutely beautiful." Told you she was lovely. "And I can really see you've got a great thing going. Such an original idea, and the eco-friendly angle is just excellent."

"Thank you, Shona. That's really nice to hear."

"Yeah, well, I was as surprised as anyone when Paul showed me the reviews and all the nastiness online. I don't want to speculate about who's behind it. I don't know if you have any idea. What I want to do is help you move forward from it, and I've got some ideas I'm really excited about."

This is sounding better and better. "Really?"

"Yes. I know Paul mentioned a couple and now you've agreed in principle, I've put the feelers out and I am sure there are a couple of magazines who would love to run a feature on Amethi. The other thing in your favour is the fact you and Julie have been friends for so long. It's a real unusual angle, and readers will love it."

"Well, this sounds amazing. We need to talk with Julie as well, of course."

"Yes, that's partly why I was ringing: I'm hoping to be there next weekend, and Paul and I wondered if we might take you to lunch on Sunday."

"That sounds fantastic... oh, hang on, I'm taking my stepdaughter shopping. We're decorating her room."

"You have a stepdaughter?"

"Well, sort of. She's Sam's daughter. I mean, Sam and I aren't married so she's not officially my stepdaughter, but it's usually just easier to refer to her that way."

"I know exactly what you mean. My ex had a daughter and a son from his marriage. We never married, but I got really close to James and Claire, and still see them once a week."

I'm finding myself warm to this woman, and feeling extra bad that I've thought such awful things about her.

"Look, no mind about Sunday. What about Monday morning? What if we take you for breakfast? Oh, I guess you'll be busy with your guests then. Brunch?"

"Sounds fantastic. I'll check with Julie and I'll let you know."

"Oh this is superb, I'm really looking forward to working with you, and to spending more time in Cornwall."

"I have a feeling it's going to be great having you here."
I actually mean it.

On Sunday, I drop Sam at Julie and Luke's, and I go on to pick up Sophie. Kate answers the door.

"How are you, Kate?" I ask, performing a surreptitious once-over. As suspected, there is no visible sign of the pregnancy. No doubt she is going to sail through the full nine months looking as lovely and willowy as ever and then the baby will just pop out, as if by magic.

"Ohhh, not so good actually." What I hadn't clocked was the pallor of her face. "This baby is giving me a run for my money. Everybody says it's going to be a boy, the pregnancy's so different to how it was with Soph. People will say anything, though. Personally, I just want to get it over and done with."

"I'm sorry, Kate, I didn't realise you were having a hard time."

"No, well, I guess I haven't been up at yours so much."

"No." There are definitely fewer people booking yoga sessions during the summer months, when our guests are largely young families. "It's going to pick up soon, though, I think. The kids will be back at school and we'll have more adult-only parties again. You'd think it'd be the parents in need of the yoga, though."

"It probably is," Kate gives me a small smile, "but who's going to look after the kids? A crèche, that's what you need! Or you could get a nursery qualification."

"Yeah, I don't think so," I grin. "I don't mind taking your kid out for the day, though. Come on, Sophie," I call, "your mum needs a rest."

Isaac pops his head out of the kitchen door. "Hi, Alice, don't worry, I'm going to make sure she rests. And I'm mixing up a super salad for lunch."

I'm sure you are. Is it my imagination or did I just see Kate roll her eyes? Don't get me wrong – I have deep

174

admiration for Isaac and his commitment to living healthily, and ethically, but sometimes I wonder if it doesn't suck the joy out of life a bit.

"We're going to get a McDonald's breakfast," I whisper to Sophie when we're out of earshot.

"Yes!"

"Though I get the feeling your mum might not be averse to an egg and cheese McMuffin, given half the chance."

"I think you might be right!" she laughs. "I am so excited about today. Mum and I did my room at home when I was nine so it's a bit young for me now."

"You've got some ideas, then?"

"Oh yeah. Definitely. Can I keep the double bed?"

"For sure."

"And can Amber come for sleepovers?"

"Well, I don't see why not."

"Hooray! This is going to be so cool!"

We stop briefly at McDonald's, Sophie wolfing down her pancakes while I work my way through an egg and cheese McMuffin and a hash brown. So bad, but so good. I swallow the remnants of my coffee and we go back out to the car.

"Where's Dad today?" Sophie asks.

"Do you know, I'm not sure. He's up to something with Uncle Luke."

"Oh they're always up to something these days. Dad dragged me over to Luke's when you were working the other night."

"Did he?" This is unlike Sam.

"Yes, he said they were working on something."

This seems a bit odd, seeing as Luke runs an IT business and Sam is a marine conservationist. They don't seem like natural bedmates.

"Weird! Anyway, you need to tell me how you envisage your room. We should have made a mood board."

"I have!" Sophie says proudly, pulling something out of her bag. "Look!"

I have a feeling it's going to be an expensive day.

As it turns out, it's just what I need. It has been a quieter week than the last one, with no online unpleasantness; none that I'm aware of, anyway. Julie said that this filter or whatever it is that the hosting company have set up managed to flag up three reviews, one of which was genuine and two of which were further attempts at malice. Apparently, one of them pointed to the fact that previous reviews had been removed, suggesting very strongly that they are linked. It's a relief to know this. I mean, deep down, I realise that these are not genuine examples of feedback from our guests but alongside all my other worries sits the one that makes me wonder if there is some truth in all of this. Perhaps I am just really bad at my job.

"That's the effect of bullying though, Alice," my dad said when I admitted this to him. "It's to make you feel bad. And it's usually done by people who are feeling bad themselves, for whatever reason."

"I just don't know who it might be. I am genuinely not aware of having upset anybody."

"That's a nice position to be in!" Dad had smiled.

"I know, it sounds awfully big-headed. But I have racked my brains and unless I've inadvertently upset a delivery person by being a bit short with them, I can't think who it might be." I've even made a list, which I keep adding to, of people I've encountered over the last year. Obviously, there are all the guests, and it's quite pleasing to count up all the people who have passed through Amethi in just twelve months, and aside from them there are the various people whose businesses we work with: Rachel, Paul's friend's wife, who supplies the flowers; Michael the dairy farmer; Clive who runs a small fruit and veg business; Kate, of course; Cindy; the list does go on. Bea is on there but while she may have been a bit disgruntled when she first found out that I was leaving the Sail Loft, I really don't think she is now – and even if she was, she wouldn't be the type to behave in this cowardly, bullying way.

I genuinely don't think everybody loves me. But try as I might, I can't come up with the name of anyone who might actually hate me. Yet clearly there is somebody out there who wants to do me some harm. It's not the best thought but I have to reason it through. There have been no threats to me or anything of that nature. It's bullying, like Dad said.

Getting away from it all and going round the DIY stores with Sophie is just what I need. It's a pleasure to be able to spend some money without worrying too much; the first eighteen months at Amethi were extremely tight and we are not out of the woods yet but now Julie and I are able to draw a little more from the business without upsetting our accountant.

Nevertheless, I have to gently curtail some of Sophie's ideas. We eventually agree on two paints; one a warm orange, like the yolk of a just-cracked egg, and then a light grey-blue.

"The orange will be the feature wall," Sophie tells me.

Did I know what a feature wall was when I was thirteen? Do I even know what one is now?

"Cool," I say, feeling anything but.

We (I mean I) buy rollers and paint trays alongside the

tins of paint, and some masking tape to keep nice neat lines and protect the architrave and skirting boards. Then we head into Penzance and go to a great little veggie cafe, tucked away from the main drag down one of the little side streets. It's busy but there's space for the two of us.

"Can we go thrift shopping afterwards?" Sophie asks, dunking a huge chunk of cheesy bread into her soup.

"Can we... what?"

"Go thrift shopping. You know. Charity shops."

"Well, why didn't you say that? This isn't America, you know."

"You did know what I meant, I knew it. You and Dad are made for each other. He's always telling me to stop sounding so American."

This makes me smile. "That's his job, didn't you know that?"

"He's very good at it."

By the end of the shopping trip, my legs are aching. We pile the bags into the car. Sophie has found a lamp and a lampshade, some fairy lights and some books, all of which are essential for her new room, apparently. We have traipsed around all the charity shops in Penzance; some more than once. "I need coffee," I groan.

"Get one at the drive-thru on the way out of town."

"We didn't have drive-thrus in my day, you know."

"Yes, I know," Sophie rolls her eyes. "I don't know I'm born. Whatever that means."

"I'm not really sure," I admit. I take her advice and stop for coffee, being harangued by Sophie to get her a smoothie.

We sip our drinks contentedly on the way home, and pull into Amethi. Mrs Jameson, who arrived yesterday, waves vaguely at us. She is putting a bottle in the recycling. I suspect she and her husband have got over-excited on their first day of holiday and started drinking way too early. It is an all-too-common phenomenon.

I let Sophie into the house first. "Hello?" I call, following her in. Luke is meant to be dropping Sam off when they've finished whatever it is they're doing. There is no reply.

I shrug. "Come on, let's eat, then we can get the room set up."

"And start painting?"

"I don't know about that," I laugh. "It's going to be late."

"But it's still school holidays," reasons Sophie.

"Yeah, but I've got to work tomorrow."

She looks so earnest, I am tempted to cave in but in my admittedly limited experience of parenting I have already learned not to promise something which you might have to change your mind about.

"Look, we'll do it soon, I promise."

"What if me and Amber come up and do it during the week?"

"I don't think so. Sorry, Sophie."

"Amber's done her own room."

"Hey, come on." I spy the signs of a sulk. "You can't really expect me to let two thirteen-year-olds decorate a room in my house, unsupervised?"

"It's Dad's house, too."

"Sophie," I say warningly, wondering what I'm meant to say next.

"Hello?" Saved by the Sam. In he comes, and Sophie flies into his arms, apparently having already forgotten the argument we were about to have. "Had a good day?" he asks her.

"The best!" She is all smiles now. He looks to me.

"It's been lovely," I say, realising I have to shake off the ill feeling as quickly as Sophie has.

"Great," he extricates himself from his daughter and gives me a kiss.

"How about you?" I ask.

"Oh, yeah, fine," he says vaguely.

"What were you doing again?"

"Nothing much. Just hanging out with Luke."

You told Sophie you were working on something, I think but I don't say a word.

We all eat together then Sam and Sophie go up to start covering furniture and checking the state of the wallpaper. I really hope we're going to be able to paint over it instead of having to strip it. As Paul had the place done up when he owned it, I'm thinking it should be in good order, and I'm pleased when Sam tells me it is.

"So I've told Sophie we can get to work," he says.

"Really?"

"Yes, sorry, is that a problem?"

"No, not at all." *Sophie, you little minx.*

In the end, we all get stuck in. We tape along the edges and corners, move the bed to the centre of the room and cover it in a dust sheet. Sam manages to convince Sophie to keep the ceiling its current shade of magnolia, rather than paint it orange, as she'd like.

It's very companionable, working together like this. It feels like we're a family. Even with the window wide open, the paint fumes become a bit too much and at some point Sophie goes downstairs. After a while, when she doesn't return, I go down to find her asleep on the settee. I get the spare duvet, which we had piled on one of the armchairs to keep it out of the way while we're decorating, and a pillow, which I manage to slide under her head without her waking. Then I wrap the duvet over her and kiss her on the forehead, turning the light off but leaving the door ajar. She may be a teenager but she's still not keen on sleeping in the dark. Plus, she may be confused if she wakes up down here.

I tiptoe back up the stairs. "She's asleep," I whisper to Sam.

"Oh no."

"It's OK, I've tucked her in. She'll be fine."

"I guess we need to finish the job we've started," he says.

"Won't Sophie be annoyed if we carry on without her? She was so into doing this herself." I am aware that I am also tired and I like the idea of falling asleep myself.

"She doesn't seem so into it now. She'll just have to get on with it, we can't have a half-painted room, and we'd have to wash all the rollers and brushes down, and the paint might dry…"

"OK."

"You go to bed, though, if you want. I'll do this."

"No, no, you've got work tomorrow."

"So have you."

"Well, we'll both just have to be tired, then."

When we finally do go to bed, I'm amazed at how much we've achieved. Sophie's walls look fantastic, though we've left the tape on for her to peel off – like a grand unveiling. She can then decide where she wants the furniture, and where she wants to put her new things.

"Damn, I didn't get her any bedding."

"We've got plenty of bedding," Sam says.

"Yeah, but not to match her colour scheme."

"Colour scheme!" snorts Sam. "She's got loads of new stuff here, she'll just have to wait, or save up, for new bedding. Can't have everything she wants just like that."

Is it possible to love this man more?

22

"Slàinte," Shona says, and she clinks her glass of cloudy apple juice against mine.

"Slàinte," I echo.

"Slàinte, Julie," Shona does the same to my friend, who's already nearly guzzled all her juice.

"Slàinte!"

Paul is watching us, a smile on his face.

"I knew you lot would get on."

"We'll have to make sure this," Shona gestures to her apple juice, "is something a bit more interesting next time."

"It's a deal," I say, taking a spoonful of the granola and fresh fruit, which has been layered in a Kilner jar, and drizzled throughout with something like maple syrup. "Mmmm… this is the best granola I've had. What?" I see Julie eyeing me. "OK, it's not 'the best'. From now on, if I say anything foodwise is the best let's take it as read that I mean 'after Julie's'."

"That's better."

"You two remind me of me and my best mate, Jack," says Shona.

"Jack?" I raise my eyebrows.

"Jackie," says Paul. "They met at uni and they are as annoying as you and Julie when they're together."

"Which is quite often," supplies Shona.

This is the most time I've spent with her and she is fun.

And really switched on. She pulls out a file with her notes in it, and flicks to Amethi.

"I know, paper print-outs. Old school, eh?" she grins. "I just have an aversion to people sitting around a table and looking at a screen – plus you can do more than one print-out." She hands them around.

The first side is a draft press release, which features a photo near-identical to the last Photoshopped one that we saw online. Minus the piles of rubbish, of course. It makes my heart stop for a moment and I glance at Julie but no, I remind myself, we already knew Shona was at Amethi that day.

"Have a read through," Shona is saying, "and see what you think. And I think we need to get you in the running for some tourism awards. I've been looking through the options and I've made a list of the ones I think you might stand a chance in."

"Won't the bad reviews and publicity work against us?" I ask.

"I don't know. I don't think so. The awards aren't judged on hearsay; there are real people who will want to come and have the Amethi experience themselves."

"Ooh, OK." This sounds exciting. I feel like Shona's already worth the money we're paying, which isn't anywhere near half as much as she charges her usual clients, according to Paul. These are things which may have crossed my mind idly, like clouds drifting across a clear sky, but I would never have thought of actually doing them. For one thing, how would I find the time?

"Shona?" Julie looks up. "When you took that photo. Did you see anybody else around at Amethi?"

"Other than Paul, no. Oh, wait, and the guy that was coming to fix the guttering."

My blood runs cold. Julie and I look at each other.

"The guttering?" I ask.

"Yeah, he was taking some pictures so that he could get the right type to be sympathetic with the look of the building. He… ohhhh," the realisation hits her.

"I didn't see anyone," Paul says.

"No, remember you were in the car, on your phone, when we first got there. Shit. Do you think…?"

"Well, we haven't had to have any guttering fixed, or replaced, or anything. Do you remember what he looked like?"

Shona thinks for a moment. "I don't. I'm really sorry. I think he had a bit of accent. Sorry, I'm really bad at English accents. Could have been… Liverpool?"

I can't think of anyone I know from Liverpool. I look at Julie and she shakes her head.

"Bloody hell, what an idiot I am," Shona says. "I hadn't even thought about that guy until now. He was just taking a couple of photos and then going on his way. He seemed friendly enough, and I remember he thought I was a guest there. He asked if I was having a good holiday. He left just after we got there. And no, I can't remember what he was driving. I'm really sorry."

"Don't be," Julie says, "you weren't to know. But that does sound suspicious. When we get back to Amethi, let's look through the booking system for anyone we've had here from Liverpool, shall we?"

"I can't be sure that was the right accent," says Shona.

"No, I know, but it's a place to start. Thank you, Shona."

"God, Alice, I don't think you've got anything to thank me for. I feel awful for not thinking of this before."

"It's fine," I smile.

"Just wondering—" Paul, who has been keeping quiet,

184

reading through Shona's handouts, looks up "—what you think you're going to do when you work out who this guy is."

I don't know. I'm reminded of the scene from *Only Fools and Horses* when Rodney is chasing down a robber. When he catches up with him he realises he has no idea what he's going to do with him, and so ends up being chased back, Del Boy of course watching from the sidelines.

"I don't think there's much we can do," says Julie, "other than giving him hell. It's not like he's done anything illegal, and even coming up to Amethi to take pictures isn't trespassing as such. But I need to know who it is."

"And I need to know why he's got such a problem with us... with me," I correct myself.

"Yep, I can understand that."

We go through Shona's suggestions in a bit more detail, then she and Paul have to get going.

"Back to the big smoke," Shona says, and kisses Julie and me in turn. One kiss, each, on the cheek – not the two air kisses I might have expected from somebody 'in PR' from London.

"I still think it could have been her," Julie says on the way back, in the little red car we refuse to give up. "Think about it... Paul was in the car on the phone. He never saw this bloke who'd come to do the guttering. She wasn't sure about the accent, or what the bloke was driving."

"No, but if that had been you or I, we wouldn't have taken any notice, would we? Somebody coming to check out the guttering. Seems plausible. And we have no interest in vehicles of any kind so why would we have noticed what he was driving?"

"OK," says Julie. "I don't really think it's her. And

actually, I think she's brilliant. I really like her."

"Me too. And can you imagine if she manages to pull off even half of what she's suggesting?"

"Ha! National TV. That would be cool."

"I don't know if it would. I'd be so nervous, I'm sure I'd look really stupid on TV."

"You'd just be being yourself," Julie smiles, her eyes on a small family of pheasants up ahead. "Move it, you stupid birds."

The baby pheasants scuttle to the side of the road while the parents stand stock-still, watching the approaching car. Julie slows down. The birds move on. "Idiots," Julie mutters. We approach a crossroads. It's left to take us back towards Amethi and right along the roads which criss-cross moorland, towards the south coast "Shall we go to that new ice cream place, see what it's like?"

"I should probably say no. I'm full up."

"Yeah, full of granola and fruit," Julie says. "Get some fat inside you, girl."

"Well... OK, if you insist."

Julie takes a left-hand turn and we follow the twisting road that winds between fields of tall, eared corn, and long rows of fat green, leafy cabbages, until we spy the sea. Even after living here for as long as I have, this sudden sight still has the ability to make me catch my breath. There it is in all its summer glory; a deep, rich shade of blue, glittering under the clear sky.

I wind down the window to see if I can smell that unique salty smell, and feel the wind on my face. The road dips a little, into a small valley, and the sea is out of sight. In the shade, the temperature drops and my arms bristle with goose pimples but I keep the window open.

"Here we are," Julie says, and we pull into a car park,

tucked in between some overhanging trees. We are at the site of an old mill, which has been restored as far as necessary for visitors to take a look around. Next to it is an ice cream parlour and behind this is the kitchen. Down here, in the dank woods, the birdsong is as rich as at Amethi in the spring. The perfect kind of place for the birds to flee to during the hotter months.

With it being a mill, there is a pond, and a stream which feeds it, then resumes its course on the other side. There is a little wooden bridge across the stream, and a few tables and chairs scattered haphazardly at the side of the pond.

Julie and I shiver and pull hoodies from the car.

"I'll get these," says Julie, "you get a table. What do you fancy?"

"Feels a bit cold for ice cream now," I say.

"Alice," she says, "this is a genuine tasting trip. We need to try the ice cream."

"OK. I'll have a honeycomb one if they do it – if not, surprise me. And a cup of tea, please."

"Ha, something to warm you up. Sure, no problem. I'll get a pot."

I sit at one of the tables closest to the water. A robin hops down right next to me.

"Hello," I say but it pays me no attention as it skips about, looking for crumbs.

Julie emerges from the little old building with a tray bearing twelve small tubs of ice cream. "I told them who we were, and that we're looking for a supplier, and they gave me these! On the house. The tea's coming shortly. I insisted on paying for that."

"Wow, so crime really does pay," I eye the colourful pots.

"Hard work pays, is what I think you mean. Now, she's

written on each pot what the flavours are, and we've got these two spoons, plus a pot of hot water to rinse them off in. Shall we both try the same flavour at the same time?"

"Seems like a good idea. Let's do it."

Julie pulls the spoons from the back pocket of her jeans.

"I think I'll give mine a rinse before beginning... no offence," I say.

"Hey. It's only my jeans pocket."

"Yeah, but who knows where it's been?"

"Doesn't even make sense."

"I know." I dip the spoon in the hot water, wiping it on the paper towel they've thoughtfully provided. The heat of the spoon after its dip means it slides easily into the ice cream, and a very tiny puff of steam rises on contact. I take a spoonful, and wait for Julie. "What's this one?"

"Pineapple and coconut," she reads off the side of the tub.

We both put our spoons in our mouths.

"Mmmmm. That is ridiculously nice. I wasn't sure if it would work with the creaminess." I take another spoonful.

"Hold on, don't fill up on this one. There are eleven more to try."

"It's hard work." I sit back in my seat, taking in the surroundings. This is a beautiful place; the lushness of the leaves; the sound of the stream babbling and bubbling merrily, against the constant background of birdsong; the depth of the shrubbery spreading across the floor of the woodland. There is the scent of wild garlic in the air, which is slightly at odds with a place that seems as if it should be all sweetness but the effect is of being in a wilderness, far away from the rest of the world. I sit back in my deep wooden seat and sigh.

"That's nice to see," says Julie.

"What?"

"You, relaxing. I don't think I've seen you sit back in a chair in weeks."

"Really?"

"Yes, you've looked tense all the time; even when I can tell you're trying hard not to."

"You know me too well."

"Yep."

"So how are things with you?"

"Oh, they're good," she says vaguely, spinning around the next pot of ice cream and dipping her spoon into the water. "But, oh fuck it, I have to tell you. I think I might be pregnant."

"What?! Seriously?"

"Well, yes, I don't want to speak too soon. I haven't taken a test yet but I'm over a week late."

"No way," I say, my imagination taking me to a place where Julie and Luke stand over a crib, cooing over their no doubt beautiful sleeping baby; or pushing a pram along the streets, to the universal approval and admiration of onlookers. Taking their child to school for its first day. Perhaps I'm getting a bit ahead of myself.

"No, well I might not be as well. But I think I feel different."

"Like… how?" I am genuinely curious. I want to know how it feels to be pregnant.

"I don't know. My boobs are sore, and I just feel really tired. So not that different to PMS, really. But it doesn't feel like normal PMS to me."

"Have you told Luke?"

"No – only you. Do you think I should do the test first and then tell him, or I should get the test and he should be there? I don't necessarily mean hold the stick while I wee on it, but be there for the result."

"I think he should be there," I say. I am flattered, and not in the least surprised, that she has told me first but I think I know Luke well enough to realise he'll be a bit put-out if I know his wife is pregnant before he does. And if she does that test without Luke, there is no way Julie will keep the result from me.

"Wow, so you're really doing this," I say.

"Weird, huh?"

"Yes, and at the same time not weird at all. How about we stop and pick up a test on the way back to Amethi, then you and Luke can do it together later?"

"I've already got some tests at home."

Of course she has.

"I just haven't felt brave enough to do one."

"Well, you've told me now, you're going to have to tell Luke, and you know he's going to want to do a test." Scientific and practical, Luke likes to know facts. He won't want to be excited until he knows that this is definite.

A pot of tea is brought out, along with two mismatched cups and saucers, and a jug of milk. We sample our way through the rest of the ice cream, saying not much more than our opinions on each flavour. Both of us thinking of the same thing, but in different ways. Julie no doubt daydreaming about being a mum; me thinking that this is going to change things, no matter how much we may not want it to, whilst also feeling delighted for my friend, and at the same time experiencing just a tinge of jealousy.

Still, it's nice to have something else to think about for a change.

Having exchanged contact details with Melanie, who runs the ice cream place, we get back in the car and head up out of the damp, dark valley – emerging blinking into the sunshine, like moles coming up through the earth.

The sea is its previous lustrous self, and the sight of it makes my stomach leap as though we have just passed over a humpback bridge. I look at Julie, to see if she shares my reaction. It appears she does, and that she also shares my thoughts: "Let's do it!"

She and I know exactly where we're going. Traversing along the narrowest of lanes, having to reverse about twenty metres at one point when we meet a car going the other way, the sun and the sea both nowhere to be seen as we make our cautious journey. It will be worth it but I'm glad Julie's driving, not me.

Again, we emerge into the sunshine; this time just above a small bay, tucked enticingly between two slabs of headland; a sliver of golden sand, topped by hard black stones, and not a soul in sight.

"I can't believe it!" I exclaim.

"I can – this is exactly how it was meant to go, today." Julie lets me out and then squeezes the car in as close as she possibly can next to an old stone wall, which oozes with delicate, tumble-down flowers. I pat the car fondly on its behind before I open the boot. It may be old but it's perfect for getting around these places; scratches and scrapes are part of its character, and we've lived in Cornwall long enough to know to always be prepared. Alongside spades and blankets for the winter are towels and swimming gear for opportunities just like this. I pull two threadbare bags out and shut the boot, slinging both bags over my shoulder.

Julie and I make our way down the steep overgrown path and arrive on the sand, kicking off our shoes, pulling off our clothes, and replacing them with bikinis. Without a moment's hesitation, we are off, plunging headlong, and head-first, into the water. Its temperature shocks me, making me gasp as I push my head through its surface, eyes stinging with salt. Julie is a few metres away, her long black hair repelling the sea water which makes her skin glisten.

"Yes!" I shout. "This is just what I needed!"

Julie laughs and ducks under the water, then swims out a little way. I follow her, my face stretched into a grin. The sun on my skin and the sea taking my weight so that I slow and turn onto my back, floating for a few moments, gazing up at the cloudless sky, listening to the bubbling depths of the sea in my ears.

I realise it's been a long time since I did this, and how much all this stupid nasty online stuff has taken over my thoughts and, even worse, my actions. I've hardly acknowledged the fact that Sam has started a new job, when I should have been showing an interest and supporting him. I can see how hard he's been working but I've been distracted from the things which really matter.

No more, I tell myself. I look at Julie, front crawling across the small cove, her arms slicing through the water. Is this it? I wonder. The time I have known would be coming, when adulthood breaks into full swing; when babies come along and force us to take responsibility for somebody other than ourselves. I often try to test myself; work out whether I could do it, but I guess, like most things, you don't know until you try.

The thought of Julie, my friend who I have known since I was eleven years old; who I've been through everything with, becoming a mum makes me tear up a little. I feel honoured to be part of her life. I am suddenly conscious of all the good things in my life – my amazing best friend, and our business; my equally amazing boyfriend, and our lovely home; my parents; my other friends; Paul, and even Shona, who I barely know.

It washes over me, this realisation, that I have all these people to be grateful for, and so what if there is one measly little person out there who's making mean comments from the safety of their computer? What do they call these people? Keyboard warriors. Too cowardly to say things to somebody's face.

I feel like the sea is restoring my strength and I swim over to my friend, meeting her halfway. Together, we swim back to shore, returning to responsibility but knowing it's possible to recapture this feeling of being wild and free, and in no doubt as to just how lucky we are.

23

Julie is not pregnant.

That very afternoon, when we got back to Amethi, her period started. I can see she is upset but she doesn't want to talk about it; wants to shrug it off and get back on with life, her vision of what is to come having altered in the space of a few hours. I force the issue, thinking that I should make her talk about it. Believing it is better to acknowledge these feelings and get them out in the open yet aware that I have not been through this. I do not know how it feels.

"It's so weird," she admits, having reluctantly accepted the coffee I've made, and the seat I've brought to sit back-to-back with the outside kitchen wall. I sit on another chair, adjacent to it, so we're not facing each other. Sometimes I think it's easier to talk if you're not face-to-face.

Julie's eyes are fixed on an iridescent green dragonfly hovering above the tall stems of yellowing grass and wild flowers which have retained their colour throughout the heatwave. "It's not that I'm desperate to have a child; or at least I didn't think I was. But ever since Luke and I stopped using contraception, it's like this feeling's been growing in me. Maybe it's like being pregnant," she laughs mirthlessly, "but with expectation and this really strong desire. I can see how people become obsessed by it, and I really badly want that not to happen to us. But just two hours ago, I really thought I might be having a baby. I really thought I was, Alice."

She looks despondently down at her cup now and it really hits me how much she wants this. Whenever I think about having a baby, it's in a fairly vague, 'what if' kind of way. I'm intrigued, rather than yearning. I feel like this is something else I've missed this summer, in my obsession over the stupid reviews and all that; how much Julie has come to be thinking about being a mum. Now, I want more than anything for this to happen. Forget the effect it will have on our working lives; we will find a way to manage, I am sure of it. I just have a feeling that there is no going back now for Julie and that this is the course her life needs to take.

I put my hand on hers, which is wrapped around her cup. She looks at me and smiles ruefully.

"I don't want to say it will happen," I tell her, "because I can't possibly know that, but you have to keep trying. And hoping."

The dragonfly flies smoothly past us, vanishing around the corner of the building.

Later that week, Kate comes to see us. Now, she is showing. Typical, I think, just when Julie's dealing with her disappointment.

"You look amazing!" Julie says to her, kissing Kate on the cheek.

"I feel enormous," Kate says. This is more like the Kate I once knew – or Casey, as I believed her to be back then. I snort. They both look at me.

"Kate, you couldn't be enormous if you tried!"

"Not on the diet Isaac's got me on," she says ruefully. "I've never wanted a Big Mac so much. And a glass of wine. I long for wine!"

The extra weight that the pregnancy has put on her is negligible but there is a definite softness to her cheeks, which have always been quite angular, and strikingly so. I actually think this new look suits her, but I know better than to say so.

Once, I think, Sam went through all this with her. She was pregnant before they got together, although she didn't know it. An unexpected memento of a brief fling with a tourist, who'd come to town in his yacht. Sam and Kate stayed together throughout her pregnancy – he was there when Sophie was born, and he was with them until she'd passed through babyhood and become a chubby, merry toddler. Then, Sam and Kate split up, and Sam moved out, but he was and is Sophie's true dad, even if biology would not tell the same story.

I am aware that in all of this, Kate has been through something with Sam far greater than I have. But it doesn't bother me now in the way that it used to.

"It's true, you look fantastic. Radiant," I say.

"Well, thank you," Kate blushes. "I just wanted to come up to talk to you about work. I am really sorry – and I can't believe it – but the doctor says I've got high blood pressure and I need to take things easy."

"That is absolutely fine," I say. "And work is the last thing you should be worrying about. Is your friend still able to take on your classes?" I don't want to give the impression that I'm only bothered about work, although it's going to be hard to find another contingency plan. We've got a yoga residential coming up, and I know a few of our guests through the autumn and into winter have booked yoga sessions.

"Yes, it's all sorted, don't worry."

"Thank you, Kate."

"It's not a problem! This is your business, you need to know everything's taken care of. I should warn you, though, Lizzie is a little bit more 'new age' than me."

"OK…" I say.

"She's on her way, actually."

"Oh, right. Well that's excellent; the sooner, the better," Julie says.

"Yes, in the nicest possible way," I quickly add. "And you know your place is ready and waiting for you back here whenever you feel ready. But no pressure, and no rush."

"Don't worry, I am going to be desperate to get back once I've had the baby, I just know it."

I glance at Julie, to see how she's coping with all this baby talk, but she looks completely at ease. "OK, but like I say, no rush. I've never had a baby myself," I laugh awkwardly, "but I imagine each one's different."

"Sophie was easy," Kate smiles. "An amazing sleeper, and just happy to entertain herself a lot of the time."

That's not how Sam tells it, I think, but it's not for me to say. Anyway, maybe Kate's new baby will be easy and no doubt she'll spring straight back to shape physically, as though the pregnancy has never happened.

A few minutes later, we hear a very noisy car engine and an orange VW Beetle appears on the driveway, its bumper shining in the sun.

"That's Lizzie!" Kate says. The three of us walk to the car park, and stand by the wall, waiting and watching as Lizzie drives into a parking space, pauses for a moment, then reverses into another one, at a right angle. "Feng shui," Kate says, and I swear she is trying not to laugh.

"From the car, a vision materialises – frizzy curly hair,

197

glowing like a halo in the sunlight; what can only be described as a poncho, and some kind of shimmering green leggings sticking out from beneath it.

"Kate!" the vision calls. "And you must be Alice, and Julie," she says, all smiles as she walks towards us, kissing Kate and shaking our hands, all the while looking around her, taking in the surroundings. "Beautiful, beautiful," she murmurs.

Lizzie is a ball of energy; we end up following her as she talks, and it's like she is bouncing off the walls, testing the place and, happily, seeming to find it to her liking. Every now and then she also makes a pronouncement, with no further explanation or apology. On seeing the red tiles, she says: "An alderman with good intentions," to which Julie and I smile and nod, then look at each other as Lizzie whirls off again. I can see Kate is trying not to look either of us in the eye but at one point she leans towards us and says, "She is a fantastic yoga teacher. People love her."

We'll have to take her word for it.

We show Lizzie the communal space – "Laughter, voices, kinship" - and Kate explains that she takes sessions outside when she can.

"I'll be doing mine inside," Lizzie says. "This place is so serene."

"OK," I say. Who am I to argue? I can't look at Julie as I just know she will make me laugh.

After a whistle-stop tour and an almost constant monologue, covering her rates and her techniques, and referencing a bookful of yoga terms, none of which I can remember, Lizzie thanks us, hugging each of us in turn and taking a moment to lay a hand on Kate's belly.

She looks around, looks from Julie to me. "A baby is coming." Seems pretty obvious to me. "A man from

Middle England isn't what he seems." Then she is back in her car and gone, the three of us standing in the dust cloud she's left in her wake.

"Did that just happen?" asks Julie.

"Yep!" Kate grins. "That's Lizzie. But she is very, very good," she says. "And she might seem like a crazy hippy, and a bit, well, mad, but trust me, your guests are going to love her."

Let's hope so, I think, but I test my own feelings towards Kate's maternity cover and find they are very positive. I just hope she doesn't scare off some of the more staid of our guests.

"Looks like that's all sorted," Julie says after Kate has gone. "Kate's being replaced by a lunatic."

"She wasn't that bad!" I laugh.

"No, she was amazing. I loved her. Totally different from Kate but she definitely seemed to know what she was talking about, even if we didn't."

"Amazing prediction of a baby, considering she's covering Kate's maternity leave."

"And what was that about Middle England? Seems a bit *Lord of the Rings* to me."

"Hmm. Maybe we should see if she'll do a couple of sessions for us, so we know what we're letting our guests in for?" I suggest.

"That's a very good idea," says Julie.

"I'll give her a call in a bit."

"Why don't you just tune in to her psychic energies?" Julie says, straight-faced.

My phone begins to vibrate in my pocket. "Maybe it's Lizzie," I say, "she could tell I wanted to talk to her."

But it's not Lizzie. "Hi, Shona," I say, turning my back

on Julie for a moment. I want to sound adult and businesslike. "How are you?"

"Great, Alice, just great. I was just checking in and actually I've got some news for you, if you're ready for it."

"Really?" It's only just over a week since we met up with her, she must be a fast worker.

"Yes, and I think you're going to love it. *Staycation* wants to feature Amethi. A two-page spread. For their winter issue."

"*Staycation*? The magazine?"

Julie's hand is on my shoulder. I look at her, mouthing "shh" while I listen to what Shona has to say.

"Yes! Isn't that fantastic news? And winter, too – just when people are thinking about booking holidays. They want to come out and interview you and Julie, and your yoga instructor, and maybe those two writers you mentioned. Mid-September, so they can get their pictures while the sun is shining – well, hopefully!"

"That is amazing. Thank you so much, Shona."

"You're welcome."

I end the call and fill Julie in.

"I can't believe it!" Julie says. "There we were thinking our reputation was in tatters and now we're going to be in *Staycation*. I think I love Shona."

"Do you know what? I think I do, too."

"There's just one problem," Julie says and my heart sinks a little.

"What?"

"No offence to Lizzie but if they want an interview with our yoga instructor, I hope Kate's up for it."

24

Having a glossy magazine coming to visit is like having an extra-bright spotlight shone on Amethi, highlighting anything less than perfect. Julie and I have been making a list of anything which we would like to fix, update or refresh, before the photographer and journalist come. We have eight days left before the interview and today is changeover day. This week is relatively quiet, being one when we have had cancellations that we have been unable to fill. Only three of the properties are rented and we decided not to advertise any late deals for this week, so that we could reduce the workload a little and concentrate on making Amethi ship-shape. Next week, we have a full house, which is perfect to show the people from the magazine.

Changeover day is here and we are welcoming back two lots of returning guests, both of whom have booked since all the online shenanigans, so I feel extra grateful to them, and determined not to let our programme of improvement works impact on their stay at all. Our list comprises details which may not bother the average guest but which I'm sure a seasoned journalist might pick up on: the lock on one of the two-beds is becoming slightly loose so we make a note to fix that; the gravel drive and paths need raking, and replenishing; the red tiles in all the kitchens need to be polished; the outside bins need to be washed out, and the compost heap turned and somehow made pretty.

Everything is doable but we are paranoid that there will be one thing we've missed. I hadn't imagined a simple magazine interview could make me go to pieces like this but Shona has been hammering home what a major influencer *Staycation* is and how a glowing feature and review from them could have people queuing up to book with us.

Sam and Luke have gone away together, to visit an old friend I've never heard of, leaving Julie and me time and opportunity to focus entirely on Amethi. Julie is pleased to have something to think about other than getting pregnant. "It's starting to drive me a bit mad, Alice, and I don't want it to."

"Oh Julie," I sympathise, "I'm sorry. I don't know what to say. I wish I could help."

"Yeah, well that would be weird," she grins.

"Ha! I guess it would."

This morning, Cindy has been and cleaned everywhere, and very kindly agreed to put in some extra hours this coming week, giving the vacant properties a deep clean. This means she'll have more time next weekend on the places which are occupied. Of course, by the time the people from the magazine come, all of the holiday lets are going to be occupied so maybe all her hard work will be undone but Julie and I are determined to get this just right.

"This is your one chance, make sure you don't blow it," Shona has told us.

Alright.

Our guests this afternoon arrive mercifully close together in time, and none of them too late. Among them are Colin and Tony, the writers.

"Hi Alice," Colin shakes my hand warmly while Tony

hangs back a little. "It is so great to be here again."

I think of Sam's semi-joke, when I was describing Lizzie to him. "A man from Middle England?" he'd said. "Isn't that Colin geezer from there? I still reckon it could have been him, you know."

Interestingly, since the TripRecommends comments have been filtered out, it has gone very quiet on that front. Nothing cropping up on Facebook, Twitter, or anywhere else that we are aware of. I suspect whoever it was realised that they were being policed once their dodgy reviews were not published. Already, all of that feels slightly surreal, as if it didn't really happen, and I can't believe what a state I was in about it all.

"Hi, Colin. Hi, Tony!" I smile warmly and lead them around to their home for the week. "You've got a nice quiet week; there aren't too many other guests, so the summer houses should be free a lot of the time if you wanted to set yourselves up for writing in them."

"I always liked the bird hide," Colin says.

"Oh, that's right. I'm sure that won't be too busy, either. And we're set for a mini heatwave, too, so you're going to be nice and warm wherever you choose. What are you working on at the moment?"

"I'm well on my way with my novel," Colin says, almost shyly, "and I'd love to bring things to a climax this week, while we're here."

"Well, Julie and I are honoured that you wanted to come back to Amethi to write. What about you, Tony? What are you working on?"

"I've got a set of short stories I'm trying to complete. One of them's the one I wrote while we were here; the one I read on the last day."

I have no problem bringing to mind Tony's sad story. "I

remember that one well," I tell him. "Well, I hope you both find all the inspiration you need here. I would love to do some writing, and I've always found Cornwall really inspiring."

"You were saying that, weren't you Tony?" Colin says. "Didn't you come down over the summer, as well?"

"Yeah, that's right, I stayed on the other side then, up near St Austell."

"Well, the whole county is beautiful, but then I'm biased."

"And rightly so," Colin says genially. "Come on then, mate, we've taken up enough of Alice's time. Let's unpack then go and get those pasties we were talking about. We fancy a little walk through town, Alice; all those cobbled streets and back passages, if you'll excuse the phrase, always get my creative juices flowing. It's a step back in time, my novel. It's... sorry, you need to be getting on, don't you?"

"No, that's fine," I think how crazy it is that there could be any suggestion of Colin's intentions being sinister. He's one of those chatty, open people who seems to like everybody. "Although," I say as I hear the familiar crunch of tyre on gravels, "that sounds like it could be our next lot of visitors."

"Go to them," Colin smiles at me.

"I will! But make sure you let me or Julie know if you need anything. And Julie's already got your menu choices for this evening, and is hard at work in the kitchen."

"Excellent, excellent," Colin is still smiling.

I welcome our next lot of guests; a couple – "Just call us Sharon and Bill" - with a toddler, who they seem to call Jammy, and, judging by the size of Sharon's tummy, another baby due not too far in the future. Like Colin, they are all smiles and ready to approve of everything. These are my kind of guests.

I show them into their two-bed holiday let, which I've brought some boxes of toys and kids' DVDs into, and they are hugely appreciative.

"Sharon's hoping to get some rest while we're here," says Bill. "Aren't you, love?"

I still have not made reference to her apparent pregnancy. I can never do it, until somebody has expressly said they are pregnant, just in case I manage to get it wrong and offend somebody who merely has a healthy appetite.

"Yep," she grins at me, "I had hoped to do some of your yoga sessions, when we first booked, but I didn't know then that I was going to be like this," she gestures to her round belly.

Surely it is now OK to acknowledge the pregnancy? "Well, if you did want to do any, our yoga instructor – Kate – is pregnant and I know is working out some routines she's still able to follow."

"You think I'm pregnant?" Sharon looks shocked and outraged.

"Oh, I'm…"

The pair of them burst out laughing.

"Only kidding," she says, "I love doing that to people. I'm due in about five weeks, but this one," she gestures to Jammy, "came early so I'm slightly nervous."

"You definitely got me there," I laugh.

"Sorry, it's a bit cruel but you should see people's faces when they ask when I'm due and I tell them I'm not."

"I'll remember that, if I ever get pregnant."

"Ooh, are you trying?"

"No, no, nothing like that. Just getting to that age, you know…"

205

"Well, we weren't trying either, were we?" Sharon smiles warmly at Bill. "It just kind of happened, you know?"

"And then it happened again," Bill's face glows as he puts his hand on his wife's tummy.

"Congratulations," I say, glad Julie isn't here for this conversation. "I hope you do get some rest this week, Sharon. Just let us know if any of you need anything."

"Thank you, Alice, we will."

Once Mr and Mrs Cooper – our other return visitors – arrive, the guests are all in and I can check off this from my long list. And with Sam away, I can work well into this evening if I need to. I am trying to prepare what I want to say for the *Staycation* interview, without it sounding scripted. Shona has been brilliant at prepping me and Julie but it's possible it's making me more nervous.

After dinner, Sharon and Bill take Jammy out in the car. "We thought we'd go into the town and have a little walk along the harbour," Sharon says. "It's stifling in the house – but not because of the house, just it's so hot," she says, flapping a tourist information leaflet at herself like a fan. "And look at my feet, they're like marshmallows," she says, staring sorrowfully down towards her flip-flopped feet.

I do a double take. Flipping heck, she's not kidding. "Shouldn't you be putting your feet up?" I ask tentatively, sure I have read, or possibly heard Kate say, that lying down with your feet above the level of your heart should reduce swelling and allow the fluid to dissipate. Mmm. Pregnancy is glamorous.

"I will, later," she says, "and tomorrow Bill is taking Jammy to the beach." She looks at once thrilled and sad at the idea. "I can't wait," she says conspiratorially, "although I love the beach, and I would love to play with

Jammy in the sand."

I do wish they wouldn't say Jammy, it sounds weird. But maybe it's the girl's real name. No, no, I'm sure it's Amelia – I did the booking. And I'd definitely have remembered if the child was actually called Jammy.

"You've got the rest of the week," I say. "Make the most of tomorrow. Julie can do you some lunch, if you like. And I can make sure we've got plenty of drinks chilling, and whatever else you fancy. You can sit outside, I'll get a sun lounger out for you, and a parasol, you'll love it."

"That sounds like heaven," she admits, and smiles gratefully. "Thank you, Alice."

"No problem."

The Coopers have gone for a stroll while there is still a touch of light left in the evening. Nightfall is coming earlier and earlier these days, and the sun definitely seems slightly lower in the sky.

I walk with Julie to the car park, both of us laden down with recycling. Colin shouts a cheery hello as we go by. He and Tony seem to have succumbed to First Night Excess and are sitting at the table outside their house, working on their collection of empty beer and wine bottles. There is definitely more drinking than writing going on over there.

"That went well," Julie says, "and those two seem to be having a good time." She gestures with her head in the direction of the laughter we can hear emitting from Colin. Tony seems quiet but perhaps it's just in comparison to his friend. "Mind if I get going?" Julie asks. "I'd kind of like to make the most of a bit of alone time at home. No offence to Luke, but it's quite nice to have a bit of space."

"Of course," I put a hand on her arm. "To be honest, I'm thinking the same way."

Julie climbs into Luke's fancy car, which he's left her to use as Sam is driving. I have the little red car should I need to get anywhere fast – at least, at a slightly faster pace than walking.

As the sound of Julie's engine disappears along the lane, I stand for a while, listening to the crickets chirruping and watching some bats flit across the darkening sky. I am aware of the murmuring of Colin's and Tony's conversation, punctuated by the occasional burst of laughter, but other than that all is quiet.

I ease my shoulders up, down and around, easing away the tensions of the day, and I sigh. I have an evening to myself now. And tomorrow is Sunday so I have nothing major to get up for. Julie and I have made sure the guests have all they need for their breakfasts. With a little bit of luck, I might just get a lie-in.

I stand for a while, resting against the solid wall at the back of the car park; the stone still feels warm, even now that the sun has disappeared for the day. Then I begin to feel hungry. I haven't eaten all that much today and now it's a bit late for a meal but I've got some good cheese and biscuits at home, and some sweet chilli jam. My mouth begins to water at the thought and I stand straight, stretching and casting my eyes across the star-strewn sky.

"Alice!" Colin calls across, "Will you have a drink with us?"

"I… well, I was just about to get something to eat, actually." Damn, I was hoping to bid them a quick goodnight and head on home.

"We've got plenty here, look – crisps and nuts, and we've opened your fancy breadsticks and humous and olives."

Why do I always find it so hard to say no to people?

"OK, maybe just a little glass of wine," I say. "Thank you."

"Go and get a glass for Alice, will you, Tony?" Colin seems very drunk and as Tony heads silently inside I'm aware that I am alone with a drunk stranger, with nobody else about, and Sam's words, and Lizzie's odd warning, drift into my mind. Don't be silly, I tell myself, and Tony is quick to reappear anyway, with a glass for me and a further bottle of wine, which he puts in front of Colin. "Just a small one," he gives me a smile as he hands me the glass then tops up Colin's. I am grateful for him realising I don't want to stay long.

They make quite an odd pair, I think. The thing they have in common is writing. But I wonder now if Tony is regretting his decision to come here with Colin; maybe this really is just First Night Excess but if they have come here to write, they can already scrub one day of opportunity off their programme. And possibly another for Colin if he's prone to hangovers.

The wine is good, though, and I sip it appreciatively, feeling its smooth warmth slip down easily. It is soon nearly gone. "Another?" asks Colin, but I put my hand over the top of my glass.

"I'd better not," I say. "In fact, I should get going soon. Thank you, though."

Shortly, I see that Colin isn't looking too well. "Think I need to go inside," he croaks, "I feel a bit..." He puts his hand over his mouth and rushes off.

I quickly realise I don't feel great, either. "I'd better go," I try to stand but my legs feel wobbly.

"Are you OK?" Tony asks. "Here, let me help you."

"No, no, I'm fine," I say unconvincingly.

"Maybe you've got sunstroke?" he suggests.

I have hardly sat still all day and I've barely been outside, aside from rushing between the various holiday lets. I don't feel like arguing, though, and accept his offer of help to get me home.

"The door's open," I croak, and Tony pushes it, supporting me through the doorway. He gets me into the lounge, where I fall onto a sofa, feeling weak.

"Could you get me some water?" I ask weakly.

"I could," he says, but he just stands there.

I find I can't seem to speak. My tongue feels thick in my mouth and I can't coordinate my limbs into any kind of useful movement.

"Alice Griffiths," Tony says, looking at me from the doorway and despite my fuzzy head I am lucid enough to realise that something is very wrong here. But I cannot speak. I slump further into the seat, wanting to say something. Tony reaches back and pulls the front door closed. My heart begins pounding as my brain tries to piece together what is happening.

"So I guess you've managed to stop the reviews," he says, disgust in his voice. "A little help from another of your mates? I wasn't wrong when I said you'd fallen on your feet, was I? Paul Winters, helping you buy this place; Mummy and Daddy lending you money; your best friend's husband sticking his nose in, ruining my fun."

Tony's face is full of anger, possibly even hate. Standing in my house, blocking the doorway; not that I can move a muscle anyway. I have never been so scared.

"I suppose you want to know who I am," he says. "Does the name Jeff ring any bells?"

"Jeff… Halford…?" I manage to fumble the words from my mouth.

Tony laughs. "Well, yes, him as well, but I was thinking of another Geoff. My best mate. Your ex-boyfriend."

Geoff, I think. *Geoff Hillford.* My ex-boyfriend. But

Tony… do I remember Tony? I try very hard to focus my mind, cast it back. *Anthony*, I think. Geoff did used to talk about Anthony. But in all the time we were together, I never met Geoff's friends; or his family, for that matter.

"I tracked you down, Alice. I found out where your parents lived, but they'd already moved away. Their old neighbour was very helpful, by the way. Told me all about their lovely new seaside townhouse, and how their daughter and her friend had started this wonderful little enterprise. Well, I had to come and look for myself. I found your website and when I saw you had a writing course coming up, it seemed the perfect opportunity. Since Emma left me, I've been writing, you see, and I reckon I'm pretty good at it."

I try to nod, thinking maybe it's best to placate him.

"I don't need your approval," he spits.

My head is spinning. I don't know if it's something he's put in the wine, or abject fear. But I can hardly move my arms and legs or form any meaningful sentences. He must have spiked my drink. Maybe Colin's too, I think, wondering vaguely if he is OK. Or maybe he's part of all this? I have no idea what's what anymore.

"What… are you going to do…?" I ask.

"Do?" For a moment, Tony looks confused. "I'm not going to *do* anything. I wanted to tell you who I am, and I wanted to tell you about Geoff, and what you did to him, and what it did to me. You need to know. You messed up his life, and you messed up mine."

He's rambling, and his eyes are wide and wild.

"You broke his heart, Alice, and then he took his life, and it broke mine. It broke me," he sobs now, white spittle forming at the edges of his mouth. "I thought I'd cracked it, when I met Emma, and then she fucked off, did to me what you did to him. Took the kids as well and they don't want to see me. She's made sure of that. Bitches, the pair of you. I thought I might do what Geoff did, teach Emma a lesson, but then I remembered you and I wanted to know what had happened. If you were sorry for what happened to Geoff but you're not, are you? Not in your pretty little house with your loser surfer boyfriend, and your nice little business."

"I'm not…" I can't get any more words out.

"I can see exactly what you are, and are not," he shouts, advancing towards me. I try to press myself back against the sofa but I'm not sure how effective that is. I feel like I'm going to black out but I can't.

My heart is pounding and my head is spinning and I'm terrified. Tony is looming over me but he's not moving, as though he doesn't really know what his intentions are. Then suddenly Sam is here, and Luke, bursting through the door and tackling Tony to the floor and I haven't got time to work out what is going on but before I slip into unconsciousness I am vaguely aware that I have never in my life been so happy to see somebody.

212

25

The day of the interview is here. I am doubly grateful for it because it's given me focus in this last week, and I've been able to think about something other than what happened with Tony.

In reality, nothing very much did happen and, if I'm very honest, I don't think it would have, even if Sam and Luke hadn't burst in when they did.

Tony is in a hospital now; a secure place where he is being looked after, and where he is going to get better. But I hope that he never comes back here. Luke, being a lot bigger than Sam, held onto him while Sam called the police. When I regained consciousness I woozily tried to tell them what was going on. I remember Sam's beautiful eyes, fearful as he looked at me. I knew I was OK but I just couldn't tell him and I fell asleep, waking to find myself in a hospital bed, my parents sitting close by, relief flooding their features when I managed a smile.

I had a terrible headache but I was OK.

"Sorry," I managed to croak.

"What are you sorry for?" Mum asked, reaching forward and stroking my hair. Just behind her I could see Dad and it looked like his eyes were full of tears.

"You've nothing to be sorry for, love. I knew you shouldn't be up there all alone."

"Phil," Mum said warningly, without turning round. "You're fine, Alice. And you will continue to be fine at

Amethi, this was just a horrible thing to happen."

"What did happen?" I remembered most of the previous evening but what I really wanted to know was why, and how Tony did what he did.

"It's very complicated, Alice, are you sure you're ready to take this in?" Mum turns the back of her hand to my forehead, like she used to when I was little and feeling poorly. "Phil, can you go and ask that nice nurse if Alice can have something to eat, please?"

Even in my dazed state I could recognise Mum's attempt to get Dad out of the room. The reference to a nice nurse is a dead giveaway; Dad is a sucker for nice nurses. He knew what Mum was doing as well as I did but he went anyway, not before giving me a kiss on the forehead.

"It's easier with him out of the room!" Mum smiled. "He's very upset. You're his little girl. I know, I know, you're not really, but in a way you are, and you always will be."

"Do you know anything about it, Mum? Where he is now?"

She knew that I mean Tony. "He's being looked after, love. He's not well. I am sure you realise that."

I swallowed and nodded.

"I've actually spoken with his mum, the poor woman, she came to see me an hour or two ago, and she's filled me in on a few things. I thought you had Geoff out of your life," Mum looked close to tears. "I'm sorry, I shouldn't get upset. And I feel awful for this young man's mum. She and his father are beside themselves. They didn't know where he was; they thought he might have done something terrible. Well, he did, of course, but you know what I mean. Are you sure you're ready for this?"

Mum's eyes were on mine, searching for confirmation that I was really OK.

"I am, Mum. I need to know, I need to get it straight in my head."

"OK, well as I believe he told you, he was friends with Geoff when they were kids. Then after Geoff... killed himself... he was in a bad way, understandably. Apparently he'd been under Geoff's spell all the time they were growing up, then he'd lost him for a bit, while he was with you. When you broke up with Geoff, this Tony thought he had his friend back but then Geoff died."

Mum paused, to let this sink in, and I was grateful, my mind still a little fuzzy, trying to fill in the gaps.

"Since then, Tony got married and has two kids, too, but his depression returned and his wife told him she wanted to break up with him. This is what his mum thinks might have triggered his obsession with you. Oh, I can't bear to think of it."

"Me neither, Mum." I couldn't believe that I've been happily carrying on with life and all the while there had been this stranger thinking about me, plotting and scheming against me.

"You have to remember he's ill, Alice. This is not rational. Hopefully now he can get the help he needs."

"Yeah," I said, dully. It was hard to feel that at the moment but I knew that I had to get to that point of understanding. As an outsider I would believe that Tony needed help.

Mum filled me in on what else Tony's mum had discovered, having managed to see her son in the early hours of the morning. As Tony had intimated to me, he had tracked me down. Apparently in his mind, I was at the root of where everything had started to go wrong for him, and wanted me to know it. It had not been his intention to physically harm me, he had told his mum. Just to make me feel as bad as he did.

My months of counselling after Geoff's death made me understand that he had an illness – it could not be seen, but that didn't mean it wasn't real. Even that morning, in the hospital, I realised that it must be the same with Tony. Don't get me wrong; it isn't easy to accept that, and it doesn't mean I don't still have a whole reel of emotions playing within me but I learned back then how to compartmentalise things, and to break them down to be manageable, emotionally and psychologically. I was terrified by Tony, in those few minutes in my house – and it really was only a few minutes – but I already know enough to realise that I don't need to be scared by him now.

He had studied pharmaceuticals and so knew what he was doing in that respect if in no other. He'd slipped something into Colin's drink to make him vomit, and in mine he'd put a lot of sleeping pills; apparently he said it was 'just the right amount' to put me into a semi-comatose state without actually harming me.

Poor Colin, who had absolutely nothing to do with this. Both he and I were kept under observation for a few hours to check that there was nothing more sinister in our systems.

"Have you seen Colin?" I asked Mum then.

"No, not yet, but Dad has. He's smiling away in his little room, making all the staff laugh."

That did make me smile. But I still felt awful for him.

Then there was a knock on the door and Dad entered, bearing a tray with coffees and a plate of toast. "And here's the hero of the hour," he said.

I thought for a moment that he was talking about himself but right behind him was Sam, whose expression whipped through a range of emotions when he saw me. I pulled

216

myself up to sit straighter. There had been enough worrying about me.

While I ate my toast, realising I was famished, Sam filled me in on his side of the story. Mum and Dad sat and watched and listened in rapt admiration.

"It's Luke you've got to thank, really," Sam said modestly. "Ever since he spoke to those guys that host the TripRecommends website he's been doing some behind-the-scenes detective work. It might not be 100% above board so let's keep it between these four walls, shall we, but he managed to find out the IP address of the person posting the reviews and then work out their physical location—"

"Geolocation," Dad puts in proudly. I could see he had heard all this before and enjoyed expanding his knowledge on the subject.

"Anyway," Sam smiled at me, "Once Luke had found out the *geolocation* we planned to go up this weekend and just have a little chat with the person trolling you."

Neither Sam or Luke are fighters so I'm not sure what they'd have done if it had got nasty so I'm extra grateful to them.

"I can't believe you did all this for me," I said, finding myself exhausted already. My eyes fill with tears.

"Of course for you," Sam said tenderly. I noticed Mum and Dad glance at each other. "Shall I give you a rest? Tell you more later?"

"No, tell me now, please," I said. "I don't think I will be able to rest unless you do."

"OK, well if you're sure. We tracked down Tony's address and went to pay him a visit but he wasn't there. His neighbour told us he'd gone on holiday to Cornwall. I couldn't fucking believe it... sorry Sue." Mum shrugged and smiled. "So we got back in the car and got back down here as fast as we could. I was driving and Luke was trying all the numbers he could think of. Nobody was answering. We tried your phone, Julie's, Sue and Phil…"

"We were already asleep," Dad said apologetically, "and had the phone on silent."

"And my phone was at the house," I said.

"And Julie had left hers in her car," supplied Sam. "The one time when an obsession with phones would have come in handy. Anyway, that's it, really. We got to you just in time to see…" He stopped.

I put my hand on his. "It's OK."

"We've all had a shock," Mum said in her typical sensible way, "but we're OK. And Tony, well it's not easy to feel sorry for him but he's in a bad way. And now he's in a good place. They'll be moving him up to somewhere closer to home later on today. Poor lad."

Dad huffed.

"Well he is. And think of his parents. Imagine if that was Alice, in a state like that."

I think it's going to take a while for Dad to feel anything like the sympathy Mum does.

"If I'd known he was actually going to do something," Sam said then, "I'd have called the police. I just thought he was a bit weird. Why didn't I call the police?"

"Because you didn't know," I said. "And you turned up at the exact right moment."

"No. The exact right moment would have been before he managed to get you to drink that stuff. God, what if he'd given you too much, he'd have killed you. You could have been allergic to it, or had a bad reaction as you were drinking alcohol, too."

"I know, Sam," I pulled him towards me, to kiss him.

218

"But I don't think we can go down the 'what if' route. I'm fine."

He put his arms around me and held me. I could hear his heart beating, fast. "I just don't want anything bad to happen to you, ever."

"I know," I smiled into his chest. "And I feel exactly the same about you."

Tony was moved by ambulance back up to the Midlands and his parents made their sad, despondent journey back home. By this time, Colin and I had been discharged and were both back at Amethi. Tony's parents came to see us both, bringing flowers and grapes and bottles of wine, and endless apologies. They looked grey and shocked and incredibly sad. I very much hope that things get better for them; to see their son in such a way must be absolutely heartbreaking. It's harder to feel sympathy for Tony after what he did but that is my aim, eventually. Mum is going to stay in touch with his parents, she says, so we can find out how things are going.

***

Julie suggested that we cancel the *Staycation* interview but there was no way I was going to allow that to happen. I didn't want Tony messing anything else up for us and besides, it's been brilliant to have something positive to focus on. I have been moved by the number of people who have been up to help; prompted by what happened with Tony. Bob and Bea have been here, Bea helping to look around and spot anything which might need fixing/cleaning/replacing while Bob has been sanding down and polishing the huge wooden table in the communal area. Mum and Dad have been as helpful as ever; although Mum has still had her job to go to, Dad has been here most of the week, being self-appointed groundsman. He's weeded the landscaped areas of the garden, and mown the paths along the sides of the wildflower meadows, twice, as well as carefully removing any sticking-out bits of hedgerow, and generally made the place look even more beautiful than usual. David and Tyler have been up here a couple of times: "We're here to offer moral support," David said, kissing me and then Julie in turn. "Don't expect me to be able to get anything useful done with this little monster in tow." Tyler was already off, running across the gravel with his arms spread wide, making plane noises. "Careful, you'll fall over," David called after him, to no response.

Even Jonathan, not famed for his selflessness, has been here on his day off, helping Julie get things together in the kitchen; little details like refreshing the spices and making sure all the pots and pans are in good working order, and shined to within an inch of their lives.

"I asked him if he'd cover for me if I ever get pregnant," Julie said when we were waving Jonathan off on Saturday afternoon.

"Really?" I am surprised she's done that without consulting me – although she knows he would be my first choice of chef after her so I'm not really annoyed – and more surprised that she's mentioned it to him. It just goes to show how much she wants it and how much it must be on her mind. "What did he say?"

"He said he'd love to but it could be awkward with Bea."

"Yes," I sigh, "first me abandoning her and then nicking her chef."

"But she can't expect him to stay at the Sail Loft forever. And Stef's still with her – and he tells me that the new manager, what's his name, is much better than you ever were."

"Really," I push my grinning friend. "The new manager is called Alex – which illustrates that Bea is trying to replicate me. Think about it… Alice, Alex, they're pretty much the same name. And Bea says Alex isn't a patch on me."

"She shouldn't say that!" Julie exclaims indignantly.

"She didn't," I admit.

For all the hard work of this week and the pressure to get things just right, I feel an enormous and unexpected relief at knowing who has been behind all those horrible reviews, and I realise just how much it was eating away at me. For all that what happened last weekend was scary, it's like the threat has now been neutralised. The thing which had bothered me the most was thinking that the person had been snooping around, taking photos. Tony has apparently told his mum that he took most of them when he was here on the course, and then he did come back that time when Shona and Paul were here, and told them he was here about the guttering. This was when he was staying near St Austell, he came all this way just to take some new photos.

As for poor Colin; he hadn't expected any of this. Julie and I said he could stay on for a further week, as nobody else was booked in the place he and Tony were staying in. He's more than happily agreed: "I'm on a proper roll with this writing now, I think I might be able to get the first draft finished down here if I do have another week. Thank you. Let me know if the people from the magazine want to speak to any of your guests, I'll be more than happy to offer some glowing compliments, and they will be totally genuine."

And now Julie and I are standing in the car park, listening to the instantly recognisable crunch of tyres on gravel, which we can hear before a gleaming car appears from between the trees.

"Just be yourselves," Shona primed us this morning. "And you'll be fine."

The car pulls into a space, on the drive which has been raked by Dad this morning. The driver's-side door opens first, and a woman gets out, her eyes quickly taking in her surroundings before they turn to us, walking towards her. "Hello!" she says. "You must be Julie and Alice?"

She is stylishly turned out, with pale-blue skinny jeans, a thinly striped open-necked shirt and pumps on her feet, large black sunglasses pushed back into her elegant hair. "I'm Catriona."

We shake hands as a man emerges from the passenger-side door. "This is Nick," Catriona waves a hand towards him. He smiles. "Hi." I can feel Julie's arm wanting to nudge me. Nick is extremely good looking, with dark hair speckled becomingly with silver, and a wide, white-toothed smile.

"Hello," we chorus, and I am stuck by the urge to giggle, like we are back in school. I manage to rein it in.

"So this is the place Shona's been telling me about," Catriona says, pulling a large bag from the boot. "Nick, grab your things, darling, I'm dying to see this place."

"You're the boss," Nick says drily, and Julie and I cast the sneakiest of glances at each other. He pulls his camera equipment from the car. "Beautiful," he says, and I see he is looking at Julie. I'm glad Luke isn't here.

"Where would you like to start?" I ask.

"I thought we'd have a look around the place, and then do the interview," Catriona tells me. "Nick can take some preliminary shots of the place then a few of the two of you while we're talking, and then some of the accommodation and kitchen, and anything else you'd care to show us." She smiles disarmingly, and I realise she's looking straight at me, holding my gaze a fraction of a second longer than I'm comfortable with.

Again, I feel Julie's virtual arm nudging me. *Do not laugh*, I tell myself. "Sounds perfect."

The table in the communal area is set out for a Cornish cream tea for four. There is also a pot of coffee, and a jug of iced water, the condensation perspiring along its sides. "Can I tempt you?" I ask, instantly regretting my choice of words.

"Not with any of those," Catriona smiles sweetly.

"OK," I say, thinking hard to find a witty riposte. I can't be monosyllabic during the interview but I swear she's looking at me with more interest than just an interviewee. Maybe this is something she and Nick do to amuse themselves.

"I'll have a coffee and a scone," he says. "Which way do you do it down here?"

We look at him blankly. I can tell Julie is also wondering how best to respond.

"Jam first?" he says.

"Oh," Julie smiles. "Yes, jam first. If you want to be properly Cornish."

"But I believe you two aren't Cornish?" Catriona asks, settling herself into a chair, and without further notice, the interview is underway. Nick helps himself to his scone, taking big bites in between shots of us, of the room, and the walls, through the windows. Dropping crumbs all over our pristine floors. He'd better not take any photos of those, I think.

Catriona is an excellent interviewer and she seems to like the place, and us.

"So you've known each other since school?" she asks and Julie expands on our friendship, and how we've been like sisters to each other.

"It doesn't put any pressure on your friendship, Alice?" Catriona pierces me with her direct gaze. I can feel my cheeks flush.

"No, not really. In fact, I think it helps that we know each other so well. And care about each other so much. But also that we have our own separate homes to go to at the end of the day."

"Ah, yes," Catriona smiles, "and you live up here, is that right?"

"Yes, with my partner, Sam."

"OK," she makes a note of this. "And Julie, you live in the town?"

"Yes, with my husband," Julie says. She looks at Nick, and he has a small smile on his face.

"She got married last year, it was a beautiful day," I start to babble but Catriona cuts me short, recognising when an interview is going off-subject.

"Sounds lovely. Now, what made you think you could do this?" she asks.

"What? Run Amethi?" I suddenly find myself filled with a will to speak well, and to stop babbling, or thinking about whether Catriona and Nick fancy me and Julie. *This is your chance*, I hear Shona's words in my mind. "I've had extensive experience running a hotel in town, the Sail Loft, which is a fantastic hotel and owned by my mentor, Bea Danson. I loved every minute of it but it made me want to run my own place, and try something a little bit different. Julie and I have talked about something like this for years and with Julie's expertise in the kitchen, and our shared belief in making a business as environmentally friendly as possible, we knew exactly what we wanted to do. It was more a matter of time and saving to make the dream happen, that was holding us back from doing this sooner."

Is that a good answer?

Julie takes the mantle. "Yes, exactly as Alice says; we've dreamed of this for a long time and talked about it so much that we knew exactly what we wanted to do. And Alice has a great feel for what people want in a holiday so adding that luxury aspect, of providing catering for holiday-makers and helping with booking days out, that kind of thing, we knew that we were offering something nobody else was doing."

"It's a bit like a catered ski holiday," Catriona muses.

"Exactly," I say, "without the skiing."

From this point on, Julie's and my enthusiasm for our beloved Amethi carry us through and I begin to really enjoy the interview. We sit and talk for another forty minutes or so and then we show Catriona and Nick around the whole site, highlighting things like our compost heap ("Not the most glamorous thing but this is essential to our use-what-we-can philosophy." I realise I have started to talk like a magazine article.)

They seem to love it all, and when it's time for them to go I find I don't want them to. It has been an absolute pleasure talking about what Julie and I are doing.

Afterwards, we go up to our office and call Shona on speakerphone.

"How did it go, guys?"

"It was great!" Julie enthuses. "Well, I think it was." A tiny shadow of doubt creeps across her face.

"It was, I'm sure it was."

"And did you like Catriona and Nick?"

"Yes, although they were a bit… flirty."

Shona bursts out laughing and I hear Paul's laughter in the background as well.

"What's so funny?" I ask.

"I knew it. They're a strange pair, and they're actually in a relationship with each other but they're well known for behaving like that. I think they get a bit of a thrill from it."

"Eugh," says Julie.

"But," Shona quickly adds, "they'll do you proud with their piece about you, I know it."

"Which one liked you, Alice?" Paul calls.

"It was… Catriona," I say stiffly.

They both explode into more laughter and I can't help grinning. "You two are as bad as them."

"Sorry, Alice, it's just I told Paul that Catriona would like you."

"I hope you two aren't getting a thrill from this," says Julie.

We hang up, and look at each other.

"One thing which has definitely been confirmed this week," I say, "is that people are bloody weird."

"And yet here we are, inviting new weirdos to come and stay here week in, week out."

"At least they're paying for the privilege."

"I suppose that is some comfort. Come on, let's get out of the office, it's so stuffy in here."

"Not long till it starts to get chilly, though," I say, a small shiver going through me as I remember the days of winter – of three woolly jumpers, and fingerless gloves, even with the heating on. The bare branches of the trees and the frost-crisp ground. Right now, it's hard to believe that it could be that cold but already there is a slight chill in the air in the very early hours of the morning, and the apples are plump and round, ripe for the picking, the orchard area buzzing with fruit-drunk wasps; a sure sign that summer is nearly done.

"Hang on just a second," Julie disappears into the kitchen and comes back out with a bottle of champagne and two glasses. "We need to enjoy this moment," she says, "and we need to make sure we always take time to enjoy and celebrate things."

"I like that idea."

We walk out into the sunshine, our shoulders touching, and I'm overwhelmed by a feeling of closeness to my friend and sheer gratitude that I have her in my life. The gravel crunches underfoot as we walk around the corner into the streaming sunshine, towards my house. We both have the same idea; tuck ourselves away in the little garden so we won't be disturbed. Just for an hour or so.

I sit at the table while Julie remains standing to pop open the champagne. "Cheers," she says, carefully pouring it into the glasses and passing one to me.

"Cheers," I echo, pushing my glass to hers. "Love you, Julie."

"You're going to love me even more later on," she grins excitedly.

"Oh yeah?"

"Yes!" she says. "But I can't tell you why."

"That is really annoying."

"I know."

We finish the bottle, my friend and I, soaking up the autumn sunshine and watching the place that we love buzz with life, from the bees and butterflies and occasional dragonfly to the garden birds, and listening to the buzzard shrieking from the line of trees bordering the land. There is a familiar twittering from the nearby hedgerow and I recognise a sound I have been missing. The blackbirds are back.

"Are you OK, after all that last week?" Julie asks after a while.

"Yes, I am, I promise I am."

"You don't think he really meant to hurt you…?"

"I actually don't. Although I think drugging me could be counted as having already hurt me. But his mum said when she asked him what he was going to do, he said he didn't know. He just wanted to make me listen. Wanted to make me feel bad. He has no idea how bad I've felt about Geoff. I guess to Tony it just looks like I've blithely continued with my charmed life."

"It makes me feel sick, to think about it. If only I'd answered Luke's call."

"You weren't to know," I say. "How could you have? Let's try and forget about it, shall we? We're meant to be celebrating, anyway!"

In truth, it is going to take me a while to really get over what happened but I don't want to think about it now.

"Were you tempted by Nick's attentions?" I ask sneakily.

"No! Although… he was pretty fit. What about you and Catriona?" Julie asks innocently.

"Ha! She should be so lucky. Wonder what they're doing now?"

We look at each other and shudder.

"With a bit of luck, she's writing up an amazing article about this place, and he's in his dark room developing his film."

"Bang up to date with your technology as usual, Julie."

"You know me."

Three glasses in, I am feeling pleasantly tipsy when I hear the front door open and close, and Sam shouting "Hello!"

"Hello?" I call back. "We're out here. And we may have had a drink or two."

"Working hard, are we?" He comes out and kisses the top of my head, stands behind me with his hands on my shoulders.

I lean back into him. "What are you doing back?"

"I've come to take you away," he says and it takes a moment for the words to penetrate my warm, fuzzy mind.

"You've…?" I look at Julie, who is smiling.

"He's come to take you away," she says. "We've got it all planned. You're going up to that place in Devon."

"Glades Manor," supplies Sam. "Where we went before."

I remember it well. That was when Sam had to dash back to Kate with her car keys, which it later turned out Sophie had planted on him.

"We thought you deserved a break."

"But…"

"No buts," laughs Julie. "Now, if it's OK with you, Luke and I are going to camp out at your place while you're gone, so that there's somebody on site."

"It's… yes, of course," I'm at a loss for words and I can feel tears welling up.

"You stay here and finish your drink," Sam says. "Julie's going to check I've packed your bag properly."

"I doubt it, somehow, but he's tried, bless him." She stands, gulping down the rest of her drink. "Sit, Alice, and chill for a few more minutes. I've got it covered."

"Bloody hell, you two," I feel slightly embarrassed and unbelievably touched by their kindness.

"Shhh," says Julie. "You can do the same for me some day."

"I will," I say, "I will."

She pours what is left of the champagne into my glass, and disappears into the kitchen, coming out with some cheese and crackers. "It might be worth eating something, to soak up some of that booze."

Sam kisses me. "Be ready to go in fifteen minutes," he says.

"OK!" I laugh and I sit with a stupid grin on my face even after they've gone inside then I begin to feel hungry and I cut a chunk of cheddar roughly from the slab of cheese, go back into the kitchen for an apple and slice that up, too. It's one of ours and it is ever-so-slightly on the tart side but its juice tingles in my mouth, just the thing to cut through the saltiness of the cheese.

I open the bag of crackers and a little sparrow which has been chirping merrily away from the gutter just above me hops down to the ground.

"Hello," I say gently.

It ignores me.

I break off a tiny piece of cracker and carefully toss it in the sparrow's direction. The little bird flutters back a short distance and I fear I've scared it off but slowly and surely it hops back towards the crumbs and when I drop a couple more near my feet it comes closer still, one of its friends joining us. A blackbird appears a little further away, at the edge of the flowerbed, weighing up the situation, but comes no further. I scatter a few crumbs on the table and the new, bolder, bird hops up there. I sit as still and as quiet as possible and soon the first bird is on the table, and a robin is watching from the fence. It, too, comes across, its bead-like eyes shining.

When I go to break another cracker, all three birds retreat but when I scatter a few more crumbs on the table, they are soon back and I hold my breath as the first bird hops across to me and alights on my hand, which is still holding some of the crumbled cracker. It pecks a little piece up, still sitting on my fingers. I can feel its tiny, delicate feet on the fleshy side of my hand, and I don't dare move, or make any kind of sound.

I can't believe this is happening and I want to call Sam and Julie to see but I know that the moment I do, the spell will be broken and so I sit as still and as quiet as I can, and time seems to have slowed down, but soon enough there is a burst of laughter from within the house and the birds flit away as quickly as they'd appeared and I am left wondering if that really just happened.

26

I sleep for most of the journey up to Devon. Sam has the radio turned down low and it's hard to describe the comfort of being there; the murmuring radio voices, and Sam's solid presence next to me. The interview now done, I realise just how shattered I am and I can't believe how lucky I am to have people in my life who are looking out for me like this. A spa break, as well!

I'd teased Sam about that when we set off.

"Ah, but I got a taste for it, last time we went, and I've been meaning to pamper myself more regularly."

"You go, girl," I said, smiling sleepily.

"Close your eyes and get some kip. Here, tuck my hoodie over you, and we'll be there before you know it. And you'll be energised and ready for some fun!"

At that point, all I could think about was sleep but I wake up somewhere on the Cornwall/Devon border and a little rush of excitement sweeps over me. "Are we nearly there yet?"

"Not far," Sam turns to smile at me, looking equally excited.

As we pull into the tree-lined drive of the hotel, I'm struck by the familiarity of the place, even though I've only been here once before. It was slightly further into autumn then, and the trees were losing their leaves. Now, they stand tall and proud, their luxurious foliage set against a perfect blue sky. I can almost feel my muscles relax just

232

from entering the hotel grounds.

We have a room on the top floor, too, with a balcony.

"They upgraded us," Sam says, bouncing onto the bed. "And this bed is amazing. Come and join me."

I do as he suggests and we lie for a while, me nestled into his shoulder, both of us letting the place work its magic. Through the window I can just make out the tops of the trees and beyond that all is blue. Swifts and swallows chase each other, screeching for joy, and I am struck by a momentary wistfulness that they will be leaving us soon for another year, but the feeling doesn't last long.

"Sam," I say, turning on my side.

He does the same, mirroring me. "Yes?"

"I'm really sorry, I feel like I've been kind of absent most of this summer."

"You haven't at all," he kisses me.

"But you've started your dream job and I feel like I've hardly shown any interest in it."

"Don't be daft – of course you have. You've had a lot on your mind, anyway, and clearly you were right to."

I see a shadow of anger cross his face. I want to sweep it away. "Let's not talk about that," I stroke his hair, and kiss him, look into his eyes. "Look where we are now. And I don't just mean this hotel. I mean, you and your job. Me and Amethi. Me and you, living together. It doesn't seem possible that five years ago I was in my little flat, working at World of Stationery, completely oblivious. Sometimes I still dream that I'm there, and if I was I'm sure I'd be fine, but I'd have missed out on so much."

"I'm very grateful to Julie for talking you into coming down."

"Me too," I fall silent for a minute. "Do you know she and Luke are trying to have a baby?"

233

"Yes," Sam's blue eyes are on mine, trying to read my thoughts. "Seems like they're having a hard time with it. But it's not that long yet since they started, is it?"

"No, I don't think so, but I guess when you want to do it, you suddenly really want to do it. I don't know, I haven't been there yet."

"Yet," Sam says, still eyeing me. "And will you want to, do you think?"

"I think so. It's hard to imagine but yes, I really think so." We have had this conversation before, but in a more roundabout way. I find myself hoping that he feels the same. It's more complicated for him, already having Sophie. "Do you want to?"

"Yes," he says so definitely that it surprises me. "I mean, not yet, but I do want to, Alice, and before Sophie gets too much older would be nice. That is not to put any pressure on you, and I firmly believe we need to spend some time together just you and me before we invite anybody else in. Just because I want to spend some proper time with you."

I smile, absolutely full of love for this man, and I pull him towards me. "I want to spend some proper time with you, too."

We have breakfast brought to our room the next morning, and we lie in bed for what seems like hours although in reality we are still up by 10am. But then all we are doing is going down to the spa: swimming; sitting in the steam room; lying back in the sauna; reading on the poolside loungers; drinking complimentary herbal tea. It's not exactly taxing. It is absolutely wonderful.

We ate in the restaurant on the first night, not talking so much but taking in the atmosphere of the grand old dining

234

room. There was a hen party in; a happy, friendly bunch, most of whom went to university together, and all clearly overjoyed to have some time together. They made more than enough noise for Sam and me, so we could sit back and relax a little, going off to bed full to the brim with delicious food and wine.

I couldn't get to sleep for a while; largely because I'd already had a couple of hours' kip in the car, but while Sam slumbered next to me I just lay back and let the velvety darkness and silence surround me, luxuriating in it. And gradually, sleep came, and I don't think I woke up once during that night.

The second night is slightly different; Sam has booked a table in the orangerie ("Where all the poshos eat.") and he's brought a suit for the occasion. "Count yourself lucky, I only usually wear these for funerals and weddings."

"Then I do feel extremely lucky," I kiss him. "And you look very handsome."

Sam had pulled out a dress for me from his bag; it's actually the dress I wore for Julie and Luke's wedding. I had pulled a face when I saw it. "Do I have to?"

"Yes," he insisted, "this is proper posh tonight, I don't want you letting the side down. Put it on, I'm going to have a shave."

Before we leave the room, I catch a glimpse of the two of us in the mirror. "Would you look at that!" I say and Sam turns. For a moment we examine our reflection. It seems familiar and strange at the same time.

"Handsome couple, aren't we?"

"Obviously," I kiss him on his smooth cheek, inhaling the scent of his aftershave. "Now come on or we'll be late."

Dinner last night was excellent. Tonight it is on a whole new level. We are greeted by a waiter who leads us into a small room to have pre-dinner drinks. I feel nervous all of a sudden, next to a group of three grey-haired couples, who look at us as we walk in. I smile at them and one of the women returns the smile.

Sam tugs at his collar slightly. "Don't do that," I whisper.

"What?"

"That," I gently take his hand away. "It makes us look like we don't belong here."

"We don't," Sam grins.

"Actually, we belong anywhere."

Pre-dinner martinis are brought to us in sugar-dipped glasses. "That is delicious," I say, licking some of the sugar from the glass."

"Don't do that," Sam says, "it makes us look like we don't belong here."

"Ha!" The other group are being led into the main dining area so we now have the small room to ourselves and I relax a little more easily. "This place is something else," I sit back, the leaves of an immaculately tended plant tickling my neck.

"I know. Sorry, I wanted to treat you, though."

"Don't say sorry! This is lovely. But you're already treating me, just bringing me here. It's perfect."

The waiter comes in, offering to take our drinks through to the table for us.

"We've already finished them, I'm afraid," I say cheerfully.

He smiles. "That's fine, madam. If you'd like to follow me, I'll take you through to your table and you can have a look at the wine list."

Madam. I want to laugh. I can't look at Sam. We are led to a tucked away table; the restaurant has been designed in such a way that there is space and seclusion for every

236

table, provided by the tall, lustrous plants which idly creep up trellises and poles.

"They must have a full-time gardener for this place," I whisper.

"You don't have to whisper," Sam laughs.

"I just feel a bit… conspicuous."

"Would it have been better if we'd stayed in the other restaurant for dinner?" Sam looks slightly concerned.

"No, no, this is amazing!"

"It's more up your street anyway, I thought, with all your fancy business networking meetings."

"You're right, I am a high-flyer these days," I muse.

"You are though, Alice. No joke. And you look beautiful." His eyes meet mine and I feel suddenly shy. I look away. "Look at me," he says, his voice all seriousness. "I love you, Alice, and maybe the start of our living together hasn't gone quite as we'd expected but that's life. Very little goes to plan, as you and I are both aware. But you stick together, and you see each other through the bad times, and you enjoy the good ones. That's what love is to me, or at least a big part of it. Oh god, I've tried to work out the right way to do this and the perfect moment but I think whichever moment it happens is the perfect moment."

He is reaching into his pocket, I'm starting to feel light-headed, and my mind casts back to a moment one Christmas time, by the fire, when he'd handed me a jewellery box. And now he's got another box in his hand, and his other hand is holding mine and he's still looking into my eyes, and he's smiling and I can't quite believe it, and…

"Alice Emily Griffiths, will you marry me?"

Oh my god. I'm shaking, I'm crying, I'm speechless.

Sam is patient, for about ten seconds. "Will you?" he asks, his eyebrows raised and an amused expression on his face.

I really, honestly, truly had not expected this. My hands are shaking and I am laughing now. Maybe I leave it a moment too long as it looks like Sam's amusement is starting to waver.

"Yes," I say. "Yes, of course I will."

He stands up, leans over, and kisses me, full on the lips. No matter that the waiter is coming over to take our order, or that one of the grey-haired men from the party who we'd seen earlier is passing on his way to the toilets.

The waiter stands discreetly back. He's seen it all before. The man, meanwhile, applauds. "Congratulations!" he says, his eyes taking in Sam trying to slide the beautiful ring onto my finger while his own hands are shaking.

"Thank you," I laugh, and I help Sam, pushing the ring on although it is a little snug.

"Does it fit OK?" Sam asks, his face a picture of concern.

"Yes," I nearly wince. "No, sorry Sam, but if we're going to get married then I should start as I mean to go on and be honest with you. No, it doesn't fit, but it is absolutely beautiful and we can put it back in its box and get it altered when we're back home."

There is a slight cast of disappointment on Sam's features, for the most fleeting of moments, then he is smiling and I don't know if I've ever seen his smile so wide. "I need a drink," he says. He looks to the waiter.

"Stop right there," says the man, who has not yet moved along. "This is on us. Waiter, bring this lovely couple a bottle of champagne, please."

"That's too kind," I say.

"Nonsense. You shouldn't have to pay for your own

238

champagne. That is, assuming you like champagne? If not, a good bottle of red…"

"Champagne is perfect," I say, and he goes back to his table to tell his wife and friends, all thoughts of the toilet forgotten. It is only when the waiter has brought over the champagne, complete with chilled flutes and ice bucket on a stand, that he comes apologetically by, whispering "Sorry, should have gone before," and practically tiptoeing past us.

Sam and I smile at each other. The waiter disappears and it is just the two of us.

"Thank god, I can relax now," he says. "That was worse than doing the speech at Luke's wedding."

"You'll have to do another one at ours," I say.

"Shit. I hadn't thought of that," Sam is grinning at me still. "I can't stop smiling," he says.

"Nor me. I thought you weren't sold on the idea of getting married?"

"So did I. But this year, while I've been back in Wales, it's been on my mind more and more. And maybe my mum and dad weren't any good at it. But yours are. And I have to admit, that was a total buzz, asking you."

"It was a buzz being asked," I say.

We clink our champagne glasses together and sit back, both slightly unsure of what we do next. I pick up a menu. Sam follows suit.

"Shall we have the vegetarian taster menu?" I ask.

"Yeah, OK. I don't really care, to be honest," Sam takes a big gulp of champagne. "In fact, food's the last thing on my mind." He sends me a look which makes my stomach flip.

"But we're here now, so we have to eat."

"I guess we'd better."

The waiter comes back and we order our food, then Sam refills my glass and we sit back while dish after dish is brought out to us. Asparagus and apple tart, followed by celeriac, mushrooms and truffle. There is sweet potato terrine, and roasted shallots with watercress and broad beans. Chargrilled fennel with olives, and chicory with beetroot and some kind of green. All of this is rounded off with coffee, served alongside orange curd and shortbread, then a slab of the darkest chocolate. We wash it all down with champagne and then a bottle of red wine. By the end of it all I feel like my stomach is about to burst.

We look for the man who bought us the champagne but he and his companions have already gone.

"Fancy some fresh air?" Sam asks.

"That is an excellent idea," I say, and he takes my hand, and we walk outside into the chill of the evening.

It's a clear night and the stars are out in their droves, the moon casting a generous slice of light across the grounds as we walk.

"Happy?" asks Sam.

"Seriously, unbelievably happy," I say. "I had no idea getting engaged would feel this good!"

"It's about all of it," Sam turns to me. "Getting engaged is a proper celebration and we'll make sure our wedding day is unforgettable but none of it means anything without a strong relationship. I know it sounds cheesy but we're definitely stronger together than apart. I want to spend the rest of my life with you, and I want you to know that, and that is why I asked you to marry me."

There are tears running down my face as I look into the eyes of this man, who I met when I was eighteen, on a beach in the town that I love more than anywhere else on earth. I am quite sure that I entertained many fantasies of us getting married and spending our lives together but I had no idea, of what it really meant, and of how it would feel. But one thing I did know was that I loved Sam, and through all the years, together or apart, I think I always have.

I throw my arms around his neck now and pull him into the tightest hug possible. "I love you so much."

"You too," he says. "I mean, I love you so much, too." Gently, he extricates himself from my bear hug, and pulls me towards the hotel. "Are you still feeling too full to move?"

"I think I could manage a little light exercise," I say.

We run, giggling through the night, towards the hotel and that enormous, luxurious bed.

27

It's party time. And no, not to celebrate my engagement to Sam. We're saving for the wedding and can't afford to blow money on a party. No, this party is for Kate, and Isaac, and their baby, which is due in just three short weeks now.

In fact, news of our engagement is not news at all any more. Disappointingly, when we told people nobody seemed all that surprised.

"Well, you're living together," said Luke, "so it seemed pretty obvious you might get married at some point. I mean, we're really pleased for you and everything."

"You're just jealous because you've had your big day," Sam said.

"You're right. I am. It was a fantastic day," Luke says wistfully, putting his arm around Julie's waist and pulling her close so he can kiss her cheek.

Julie was not surprised at all because she was the one person Sam had shared his plan with. She was, however, the most excited out of everybody and was waiting on the car park at Amethi when we got back from Glades Manor.

"Well?" she exclaimed. "Where is it?" Clearly she had no doubt that I would have said yes. Cruelly, I displayed my bare finger to her, and her face fell momentarily until she saw the huge smile on my face.

"It was too small!" I shouted, and dashed out of the car towards her, across the gravel, where we hugged and jumped about while Sam watched from a safe distance.

"I do sometimes wonder if it shouldn't have been you two getting married," he said.

"I would have but she's too ugly," I squeezed my friend's hand, reaching out my other arm for Sam and together we walked back into the warm embrace of Amethi. I took a moment to consider my ridiculously good fortune, flanked either side by these two people I love.

Mum and Dad were equally unsurprised but just as delighted as Julie.

"Hey, what happened to asking me first?" Dad said.

"You're already married, Phil," said Sam.

"Ha. For my permission, I meant."

"I didn't think Alice was the kind of person who'd want me to ask for permission from anyone but her," Sam smiled at me.

"You're right, I'm not."

"But do I still get to walk you down the aisle?" Dad asked eagerly.

"We haven't really given any thought to the wedding yet." Seeing Dad's crestfallen expression, I added quickly, "But whatever we do, I am going to need you to be a big part of it, Dad. And I might not want to be given away. But I also don't know if I want to take Sam's surname. I think I'd like to keep mine, and yours. I don't know. Maybe we'll change our minds about all these things; probably more than once, in fact."

"As long as you don't elope," Mum said, quickly adding, "I mean, it should be whatever you two want. It's your wedding. If you want to go and get married abroad with strangers for witnesses, then that's what you should do."

I know that's the last thing Mum really thinks.

"That's not very likely, Mum," I said, and relief flooded her face, although she did her best to hide it.

There was more champagne that afternoon and again, when we told Sophie and then Kate.

Sophie was delighted. "You're going to be my stepmum!" she said, hugging me. "That is seriously good news, you two," Kate said, her hands resting on her not inconsiderable bump.

I was really pleased with Sophie's reaction. She's got a lot going on at the moment, with becoming a sister, and it's not been that long since Isaac moved in with her and Kate.

"As long as you don't have a baby straight away and kick me out of my room," she smiled.

"Sophie!" Kate said warningly but I just laughed.

"I think it's a bit soon for that, Sophie," I said. "We haven't even set a wedding date yet. And your room is *your* room, don't forget it."

Yet more champagne was to come, when we told David and Martin. David rang Bea and made me tell her, and invite her and Bob over for an impromptu celebration.

I began to think I could get used to that lifestyle but before long everything was back to normal as work took over once more.

Today's celebration is nothing to do with us and it's actually a pleasant change. Isaac has arranged a light lunch in the Mainbrace pub; amazing that he hasn't gone for the wholefood café in Penzance but apparently Kate put her foot down about this.

Sam and I park at the top of the hill, walking down the steep sets of steps and through the twisting narrow streets to get there. I realise just how much I have missed being in town; even when I come to see Mum and Dad it's normally a quick in and out, to their house and back.

I used to love wandering through the meandering streets and tangle of passageways and I determine that I will come down at Christmas, which is not all that far off now, and spend a bit of time just being here. This place has a lot of memories for me and though I love Amethi to bits, it was this town which I became attached to that first golden summer with Julie. While I haven't forgotten its magic I realise I haven't given it enough time at all over this last year or so.

"Can we have a little walk before we go in?" I ask Sam.

"Erm, yeah," he looks at his watch doubtfully.

"Just a short one," I plead. "Along behind the beaches. It'll take fifteen minutes, tops."

"Go on then."

So we walk, hand in hand, the wind from across the sea casting a rosy glow on our cheeks. It is not fully winter yet but it's cold enough for coats these days and the town is quieter now than even just a few weeks ago. There are signs for firework displays this coming weekend.

The tide is in and as we follow the walkway along the very bottom of town; taking us away from the harbour and towards the train station, waves crash below us, firing spouts of foam into the air. As we walk, turnstones scatter out of the way on their spindly orange legs, gathering behind us again once we've passed.

"I love it here so much," I say to Sam.

"I know," he kisses me. "More than Amethi?"

"No, not more, I don't think. But differently."

"I know what you mean."

"It's wild, here. It makes me feel alive in a way nowhere else does."

"But you don't feel unhappy at Amethi?"

"God, no."

"Even after Tony…?"

"Even after Tony," I confirm.

I have surprised myself by how little I've been affected by all that. I test myself from time to time, to try and make sure I'm not fooling even myself, but I really don't think I am. His mum and my mum have kept in touch; possibly become friends, even. Tony is living back with her and his dad now and is doing quite well, apparently. He wanted to write and apologise but I asked Mum to tell his mum that I didn't want that. I just want to forget it. I feel sorry for him, but I don't ever want to hear from him again. Hard though it may sound, it is his responsibility to sort himself out.

We walk on, Sam and I, and I relish the feeling of the onset of winter. There is always a brief time when I enjoy getting out my woolly jumpers, coats and boots, and that time is now. I am sure the novelty will wear off soon and by February I will be impatient for some sunshine and warmth. Maybe this year Sam and I should go somewhere hot in January. An all-inclusive holiday, where I get to ask other people to do things for me.

That is not for now, though. We walk as far as the beach by the station. The clouds hang low in the sky over the sea and the town, giving the place a cosiness at odds with the wild abandon of summer. I want to go on but Sam is getting agitated.

"Come on," I say. "I know, we need to get to the party." I long to be able to just spend the afternoon walking – go up on the coast path, though it's likely to be much windier up there – but this is not my afternoon. It is Kate's, and Isaac's, and Sophie's. They are Sam's family still and so by

246

extension they are mine.

We walk back to the pub, Sam with his arm around my shoulders, and by the time we get in there I find my teeth are chattering. As soon as we open the door, we are greeted by the warmth of the open fire and a great group of people who have come to celebrate Kate's pregnancy. Julie and Luke are already at a table so I head towards them, distracted momentarily by a gale of laughter from the other side of the bar. It is Isaac, and if I'm not very much mistaken, he is drunk. Kate is standing nearby, casting a wary, almost embarrassed, look towards him. I turn to look at Julie, who grins and makes the international gesture for 'he's had a few too many'. Perhaps this is the reason Isaac turned obsessively healthy; maybe he just can't handle his drink.

I'm glad we are not any later because, while Sam goes to the bar, Sophie immediately glueing herself to his side, there is the *ting, ting* of a spoon being knocked against a glass, commanding the attention of everybody in the room. I stand next to Julie and we look expectantly towards Isaac, who is swaying slightly and waiting for silence.

"Thanks for coming, everybody," he says. "I will keep this brief. I know a baby shower isn't a traditional thing to do and we didn't want one in the American sense of the word but we did want to get as many people we care about together, today. In a few weeks' time my beautiful Kate will be giving birth to our baby and as its life begins, our new life as a family will. And we're already a family, of course, having Sophie," I look across to her and see how she's taking this. She doesn't look too delighted and I can see Sam's not overly impressed either but there is more to come. "And with that new life, Kate and I have decided it's time for a proper new start. We've been keeping this under wraps until we've got all the details sorted but the papers came through yesterday and we are now the proud owners of a yoga retreat."

There are whistles and cheers at this news. I glance towards Sam and Sophie again, both of whom look surprised at the news. Kate, too, looks shocked, as though she hadn't expected him to be saying all this.

"Thank you," Isaac continues, gesturing for people to quieten down. "We'll be taking it over in the spring, if all goes to plan, once we've had a bit of time to get used to being parents."

"Well, I'm already a parent," Kate interjects, with an air of forced joviality.

"Yes, of course," Isaac says hurriedly. "And Sophie you know I think of you as a daughter. Not," he fumbles with his words, "in your place, Sam, of course."

My toes are curling inside my boots. Poor Isaac, he's going to regret all this later, if he remembers it. I can't look at Julie because I know she'll make me laugh. Instead, I steal a glance at Luke, who is staring into his pint glass.

"Where's the yoga centre?" somebody calls and I see Isaac falter, perhaps seeing his error in announcing the news this way but realising that there is no backtracking now. At this very moment, a couple of bar staff move out from behind the bar, expertly carrying trays bearing glasses of Buck's Fizz and plain orange juice, moving smilingly from guest to guest.

"It's, erm, in Devon," Isaac says, into an otherwise silent room.

Sophie gasps and runs from the room. Sam is hot on her heels.

Kate looks as though she'd like to throttle Isaac. She stands to go after her daughter but gasps sharply and sits straight back down. Isaac turns and crouches next to her but she pushes him away. Now the room is truly silent then Lizzie, of all people, makes her way over to Kate.

"Are you OK, my lovely?"

Kate whispers something to her.

"Oh," says Lizzie, looking down, then she says it again, as though something has clicked. "*Oh.*"

She moves people gently but authoritatively aside, sending Isaac to speak to the landlord. A space is cleared around Kate, who looks both furious and anxious, and extremely flushed.

I watch from across the room, wondering whether to go and see if she's OK, or to follow Sam and Sophie. There is not a lot of space to move either way so I stand where I am for now, watching and waiting. People are politely accepting the glasses from the bar staff, who look like they are now aware they've walked into the middle of something but seem to have decided they have no option but to fulfil their destiny and make sure everybody has a drink. The soft murmur of conversation begins again.

Julie stands up and leans towards me. "What the fuck?" she whispers. "Did you know about this?"

"No," I say grimly, "and apparently neither did Sam or Sophie."

"Do you want to go to them?"

"I think they're better left to themselves right now," I say. "Sophie probably just needs her dad for the time being."

I look across to see what Kate is doing but she is nowhere to be seen, and neither is Isaac.

A barmaid appears at my elbow, proffering glasses. "Thank you," I smile, taking two and handing one to Julie. Luke accepts a glass too, smiling at the barmaid. He looks at me and raises his eyebrows. I shrug my shoulders.

The landlord rings the bell and the room falls silent once more.

"Ladies and gents," he calls, "Kate and Isaac have asked me to tell you to enjoy yourselves this afternoon. It seems Kate's, erm, *waters have broken…*"

He practically whispers these last words and some joker shouts, "Speak up!"

The landlord is rescued by the barmaid. "It looks like Kate is going into labour," she says loudly. "She's gone out the side door, and said to tell you all to stay as long as you like. They've paid for a few more bottles of this stuff," she waves a bottle of champagne in the air, "so you might as well make the most of it! But first off, a toast. To Kate, and Isaac, and their new baby."

I am really glad Sophie is not here to hear this. And god knows what Isaac's going to be like in the delivery room; after all his careful planning and structured birthing plan, he's going to be drunk for the birth of his first child. I shouldn't be glad and I'm not really but I am incredibly angry at him for what he's just done and I can't help but feel this is his comeuppance. Poor Kate, though. I check for Lizzie, who is also nowhere to be seen. Imagine giving birth with New Age Lizzie and Drunk Isaac for support. I shudder.

As we raise our glasses, I look at Julie, hoping she can't tell mine is just orange juice.

"To Kate and Isaac, and their new baby," we chorus dutifully.

I take a sip of my drink and my free hand moves tentatively, cautiously, towards my stomach. I've also got something I haven't yet told anybody but I don't think now is the time to do so.

Thank you very much for taking the time to read
Sticks and Stones

If you've enjoyed this book, a positive review on Amazon
or Goodreads would be much appreciated.

In case you missed Books One to Three...

A Second Chance Summer

Alice knows that coming back to Cornwall means she will have to see Sam, the man she fell in love with aged 18.

How will he react to her return, and what changes have the intervening ten years meant for them both?

Still recovering from a toxic relationship, Alice realises she has allowed life to become too predictable, while Julie has just ended things with the man she was due to marry. The two friends decide to throw caution to the wind; coming back to Cornwall, where they spent a long, happy summer before life got serious. As they return to the same small flat in the centre of town, and seasonal jobs at the Sail Loft Hotel, Alice harbours both hopes and fears of finding Sam, while Julie is determined to enjoy the freedom she's been missing.

After the Sun

Sam and Alice, only recently reunited, face separation when Sam's only option in order to continue his studies is to leave Cornwall while Alice is committed to her new job managing the Sail Loft Hotel in landlady Bea's absence.

Sam's visits see him split in his loyalties between his daughter Sophie, and spending time with Alice. Sophie's mother, Kate, seems to be doing her best to make things difficult.

Meanwhile, Alice's friend Julie faces a similar challenge as her new partner, and Sam's best friend, Luke, is working in London. Struggling to keep herself in work now the summer season has ended, Julie has some big decisions to make.

Can these fledgling relationships pass the long-distance test, and can Julie and Alice make life in Cornwall work for them now that the summer sun has gone?

As Boundless as the Sea

Two years into her new life in Cornwall, and while Alice Griffiths' own romantic hopes have been dashed, it appears that whichever way she looks, her friends are getting hitched.

A handsome stranger at Bea's wedding could well change Alice's fortunes but she may be better off ploughing her energies into her working life.

While each season brings a new wedding, the months leading up to Christmas, and David and Martin's big day, become about taking risks for Alice. Should she leave the safety of the Sail Loft Hotel? Is starting a business the best idea she and Julie have ever had, or the end of a beautiful friendship? And should she push Sam Branvall out of her mind for good and take a chance on handsome, successful Paul Winters?

From upsetting her manager at the Sail Loft, to Sam moving back to town; not to mention a phone call announcing her mother has been taken seriously ill, it's going to take a cool head to navigate successfully through this year. Luckily, Alice has her friends to support her. Even if they are all getting married.

If she can just keep her cool, and keep her friends, then she should make it safely through to those cold winter nights and twinkling Christmas lights.

Acknowledgements

First and foremost I have to thank everybody who has bought, read and hopefully enjoyed the Coming Back to Cornwall series, and encouraged me to write a fourth. This year has been incredible for me so far and I am very grateful to you all.

I had not planned this fourth instalment; in fact, I had not planned this series at all, but as I have mentioned before, inspiration struck whilst on holiday in Cornwall in 2017. I have become extremely fond of Alice, Julie, Sam, Luke and (most of) the rest of the characters in this series. I've really enjoyed writing each book and I'm very happy to say that there is one more to come…

I owe a HUGE thank you to my amazing friend Catherine Clarke, who never fails to produce beautiful, eye-catching covers, for myself and a lot of the other authors at Heddon Publishing. She is multi-talented, and I feel that our paths were destined to cross. Let's hope she's as happy about that as I am.

A special thank you is due to my beta reading team, which has grown significantly this year. Thanks to every one of you for taking the time to read *Sticks and Stones*, and send me your thoughts. In no particular order, thank you Helen Smith, Jean Thomas, Myra Hall, Louise Freeman, Wendy Pompe, Denise Armstrong, Katie Copnall, Jenny Holdcroft,

Patricia Aspley, Janet Evans, Clare Coburn, Hilary Kerr, Mary Tolcher, and Claudia Baker.

This list includes friends I have made recently, friends I have never (yet) met in person, and one friend I have known for a long, long time. Claudia is the first person I sat next to at primary school and we were pretty much inseparable until my family and I moved to Bristol just before I began secondary school. We kept in touch for quite a while and then met up again some years later and quite by chance have both ended up living in Shropshire. It's a huge pleasure to be able to meet up with her again and an honour to have my audio-book-loving friend beta reading for me!

Finally, as ever, I must thank my dad, Ted Rogers, who has read this book twice already and offered some excellent feedback and advice.

I sincerely hope I have not missed anybody from my list but if I have it is a genuine mistake and you must let me know!

Writing the Town Read

You can currently get an ebook of *Writing the Town Read* for FREE on Katharine's website: www.katharineesmith.com.

On July 7th 2005, terrorists attack London's transport network, striking Underground trains and a bus during the morning rush hour. In Cornwall, journalist Jamie Calder loses contact with her boyfriend Dave, in London that day for business.

The initial impact is followed by a slow but sure falling apart of the life Jamie believed was settled and secure. She finds she has to face a betrayal by her best friend, and the prospect of losing her job.

Writing the Town Read is full of intrigue, angst, excitement and humour. The evocative descriptions and convincing narrative voice instantly draw readers into Jamie's life as they experience her disappointments, emotions and triumphs alongside her.

Looking Past

Sarah Marchley is eleven years old when her mother dies. Completely unprepared and suffering an acute sense of loss, she and her father continue quietly, trying to live by the well-intentioned advice of friends, hoping that time really is a great healer and that they will, eventually, move on.

Life changes very little until Sarah leaves for university and begins her first serious relationship. Along with her new boyfriend comes his mother, the indomitable Hazel Poole. Despite some misgivings, Sarah finds herself drawn into the matriarchal Poole family and discovers that gaining a mother figure in her life brings mixed blessings.

Looking Past is a tale of family, friendship, love, life and death – not necessarily in that order.

Amongst Friends

Set in Bristol, *Amongst Friends* covers a period of over twenty years, from 2003 all the way back to 1981. The tone is set from the start, with a breathtaking act of revenge, and the story winds its way back through the key events which have led the characters to the end of an enduring friendship.

Both of Katharine's first two novels are written from a strong female first-person perspective. Amongst Friends takes her writing in a different direction, as the full range of characters' viewpoints are represented throughout the story.

How to Run a Free Kindle Promotion on a Budget

Written primarily for other indie authors, this is a great guide to making the most of your 'free days' in the Kindle Direct Publishing KDP Select programme.

With BookBub deals hard to come by, not to mention pricey, *How to Run a Free Kindle Promotion on a Budget* takes you step-by-step through the process, from planning to record-keeping. It also includes real examples to illustrate the success or otherwise of the techniques described.